REA's Test Prep Books Are The Best!

(a sample of the <u>hundreds of letters</u> REA receives each year)

" Pass the CLEP Principles of Marketing with points to spare...
I'm definitely not a business whiz, yet I came in scoring in the top percentile
using this book... REA and the authors have done an exceptional job. "
A CLEP Principles of Marketing Test-Taking Student

" My students report your chapters of review as the most valuable single
resource they used for review and preparation. "
Teacher, American Fork, UT

" Your book was such a better value and was so much more complete than
anything your competition has produced — and I have them all! "
Teacher, Virginia Beach, VA

" Compared to the other books that my fellow students had, your book was
the most useful in helping me get a great score. "
Student, North Hollywood, CA

" Your book was responsible for my success on the exam, which helped me get
into the college of my choice... I will look for REA the next time I need help. "
Student, Chesterfield, MO

" Just a short note to say thanks for the great support your book gave me in
helping me pass the test... I'm on my way to a B.S. degree because of you! "
Student, Orlando, FL

(more on next page)

(continued from front page)

" I just wanted to thank you for helping me get a great score
on the AP U.S. History exam... Thank you for making great test preps! "
Student, Los Angeles, CA

" Your *Fundamentals of Engineering Exam* book was the absolute best
preparation I could have had for the exam, and it is one of the major
reasons I did so well and passed the FE on my first try. "
Student, Sweetwater, TN

" I used your book to prepare for the test and found that the advice and the
sample tests were highly relevant... Without using any other material, I earned
very high scores and will be going to the graduate school of my choice. "
Student, New Orleans, LA

" What I found in your book was a wealth of information sufficient to shore up
my basic skills in math and verbal... The section on analytical ability was
excellent. The practice tests were challenging and the answer explanations most
helpful. It certainly is the *Best Test Prep for the GRE*! "
Student, Pullman, WA

" I really appreciate the help from your excellent book. Please keep up
the great work. "
Student, Albuquerque, NM

" I am writing to thank you for your test preparation... your book helped me
immeasurably and I have nothing but praise for your *GRE* preparation."
Student, Benton Harbor, MI

(more on back page)

THE BEST TEST PREPARATION FOR THE

CLEP

PRINCIPLES OF MARKETING

5th EDITION

New Practice Test Material by

Anindya Chatterjee, Ph.D.
Slippery Rock University
Slippery Rock, PA

James E. Finch, Ph.D.
Chairperson, Department of Marketing
University of Wisconsin, La Crosse, WI

James R. Ogden, Ph.D.
Chairperson, Department of Marketing
Kutztown University, Kutztown, PA

Denise T. Ogden, Ph.D.
Assistant Professor in Marketing/Busniess Administration
Penn State Berks/Lehigh Valley College, Reading/Fogelsville, PA

Research & Education Association
61 Ethel Road West
Piscataway, New Jersey 08854

**The Best Test Preparation for the
CLEP PRINCIPLES OF MARKETING**

ABOUT OUR AUTHORS

James Finch is the director of the M.B.A. program at the University of Wisconsin–La Crosse. He has also served the university as interim associate dean of the College of Business Administration and as a graduate faculty member. Dr. Finch holds a Ph.D. from Ohio State University.

James Ogden is the chair of the Department of Marketing at Kutztown University in Kutztown, Pennsylvania. He has formerly taught at Cedar Creek College, Central Michigan University, and the University of Northern Colorado, among others. Dr. Ogden received his Ph.D. in College Student Personnel Administration from the University of Northern Colorado, and his M.S. in Marketing from Colorado State University.

Denise Ogden is an assistant professor in Marketing/Business Administration at Penn State Lehigh Valley in Reading/Fogelsville, Pennsylvania. She has also taught at Allentown College/DeSales University and Cedar Crest College. Dr. Ogden holds a Ph.D. in Business Administration from Temple University.

Anindya Chatterjee is an associate professor of Marketing at Slippery Rock University in Slippery Rock, Pennsylvania. He has previously taught at Temple University, from which he received a Ph.D. in Marketing.

ABOUT RESEARCH & EDUCATION ASSOCIATION

Founded in 1959, Research & Education Association (REA) is dedicated to publishing the finest and most effective educational materials—including software, study guides, and test preps—for students in middle school, high school, college, graduate school, and beyond.

REA's Test Preparation series includes study guides for all academic levels in almost all disciplines. Research & Education Association publishes test preps for students who have not yet completed high school, as well as high school students preparing to enter college. Students from countries around the world seeking to attend college in the United States will find the assistance they need in REA's publications. For college students seeking advanced degrees, REA publishes test preps for many major graduate school admission examinations in a wide variety of disciplines, including engineering, law, and medicine. Students at every level, in every field, with every ambition can find what they are looking for among REA's publications.

REA's publications and educational materials are highly regarded and continually receive an unprecedented amount of praise from professionals, instructors, librarians, parents, and students. Our authors are as diverse as the subject matter represented in the books we publish. They are well-known in their respective disciplines and serve on the faculties of prestigious universities throughout the United States and Canada.

ACKNOWLEDGMENTS

In addition to our authors, we would like to thank Larry B. Kling, Vice President, Editorial Services, for his overall direction; Robert Coover and Diane Goldschmidt, Associate Editors, for coordinating revisions for this new edition; Pam Weston, Vice President, Publishing, for ensuring press readiness; Jeremy Rech, Graphic Artist, for his production support and Wende Solano and Network Typesetting, Inc., for typesetting the manuscript.

CONTENTS

INDEPENDENT STUDY SCHEDULE

INDEPENDENT STUDY SCHEDULE
CLEP PRINCIPLES OF MARKETING CBT

The following study schedule allows for thorough preparation for the CLEP Principles of Marketing. Although it is designed for six weeks, it can be reduced to a three-week course by collapsing each two-week period into one. Be sure to set aside enough time—at least two hours each day—to study. But no matter which study schedule works best for you, the more time you spend studying, the more prepared and relaxed you will feel on the day of the exam.

Week	Activity
1	Read and study Chapter 1, which will introduce you to the CLEP Principles of Marketing. Then take Practice Test 1 to determine your strengths and weaknesses. Score your exam by using the score chart found in Chapter 1. You can then determine the areas in which you need to strengthen your skills.
2 & 3	Carefully read and study the Principles of Marketing review included in this book.
4	Take Practice Test 2, and after scoring your exam, review carefully all incorrect answer explanations. If there are any types of questions or particular subjects that seem difficult to you, review those subjects by studying again the appropriate section of the Principles of Marketing review.
5	Take Practice Test 3, and after scoring your exam, review carefully all incorrect answer explanations. If there are any types of questions or particular subjects that seem difficult to you, review those subjects by studying again the appropriate section of the Principles of Marketing review.
6	Study any areas you consider to be your weaknesses by using the Principles of Marketing Review and any other study resources you have on hand. You may want to retake the practice tests using the extra answer sheets provided in the back of this book.

CHAPTER 1
PASSING THE CLEP
PRINCIPLES OF
MARKETING CBT

Chapter 1

PASSING THE CLEP PRINCIPLES OF MARKETING CBT

ABOUT THIS BOOK

This book provides you with comprehensive preparation for the CLEP Principles of Marketing CBT. Inside you will find a concise review of material typical of a one-semester introductory course in marketing, as well as tips and strategies for test-taking. We give you three full-length REA practice tests, all based on the official CLEP subject exam. Our practice tests contain every type of question that you can expect to encounter on the CLEP CBT. Following each practice test you will find an answer key with detailed explanations designed to help you more completely absorb the test material.

ABOUT THE EXAM

Who takes CLEP exams and what are they used for?

CLEP (College-Level Examination Program) examinations are usually taken by adults who have acquired knowledge outside the classroom and wish to bypass certain college courses and earn college credit. The CLEP Program is designed to reward students for learning—no matter where or how that knowledge was acquired. The CLEP is the most widely accepted credit-by-examination program in the country, with more than 2,900 colleges and universities granting credit for satisfactory scores on CLEP exams.

Although most CLEP candidates are adults returning to college, many graduating high school seniors, enrolled college students, and international students also take the exams to earn college credit or to demonstrate their ability to perform at the college level. There are no prerequisites, such as age or educational status, for taking CLEP examinations. However, because policies on granting credits vary among colleges, you should contact the particular institution from which you wish to receive CLEP credit.

There are two categories of CLEP examinations:

1. **CLEP General Examinations**, which are five separate tests that cover material usually taken as requirements during the first two years of college. CLEP General Examinations are available for English Composition (with or without essay), Humanities, Mathematics, Natural Sciences, and Social Sciences and History.

2. **CLEP Subject Examinations**, which include material usually covered in an undergraduate course with a similar title. The CLEP Principles of Marketing CBT is one of 29 subject examinations.

Who develops and administers the exams?

The CLEP is developed by the College Entrance Examination Board, administered by Educational Testing Service, and involves the assistance of educators from across the United States. The test development process is designed and carried out to ensure that the content and difficulty of the test are appropriate to the college level.

When and where is this exam given?

The CLEP Principles of Marketing exam is administered each month throughout the year at more than 1,400 test centers in the U.S. and can be arranged, on request, for candidates abroad. To find the test center nearest you and to register for the exam, you should obtain a copy of the free booklets *CLEP Colleges* and *CLEP Information for Candidates and Registration Form*. These booklets are downloadable and are available at most colleges where CLEP credit is granted, or by contacting the CLEP Program at:

CLEP Services
P.O. Box 6601
Princeton, NJ 08541-6601
Phone: (609) 771-7865
Website: *http://www.collegeboard.com*

Military personnel and CLEP

CLEP exams are available free-of-charge to eligible military personnel and eligible civilian employees. The College Board has developed a paper-based version of 14 high volume/high pass rate CLEP tests for DANTES Test Centers. Contact the Educational Services Officer or Navy College Education Specialist for more information. You can also visit Collegeboard.com for details about CLEP opportunities for military personnel.

HOW TO USE THIS BOOK

What do I study first?

It's best to read over the course review, along with our suggestions for test-taking, first. Then take Practice Test 1 to pinpoint your area(s) of weakness.

For details on how to utilize your study time, follow our Independent Study Schedule in the front of this book. The schedule is based on a six-week program, but can be condensed to three weeks if necessary by collapsing each two-week period into one.

In effect, this book offers a blueprint for how to put yourself in the best possible position for success on the CLEP CBT. Follow it all the way the through, and you'll be well on your way to a good score!

When should I start studying?

It's never too early to start studying for the CLEP Principles of Marketing exam. The earlier you begin, the more time you will have to sharpen your skills. Do not procrastinate! Last-minute cramming is *not* an effective way to study, since it does not allow you the time needed to learn the test material. The sooner you learn the format of the exam, the more time you will have to familiarize yourself with it.

FORMAT AND CONTENT OF THE CLEP CBT

The CLEP Principles of Marketing CBT covers material that is usually taught in an introductory college course in marketing. This type of course is commonly known as Basic Marketing, Introduction to Marketing, Fundamentals of Marketing, Marketing, or Marketing Principles. Such a course—and thus, the exam itself—covers the role of marketing in society and within a firm, understanding consumer and organizational markets, marketing strategy planning, marketing institutions, the marketing mix, as well as topics like international marketing, ethics, marketing research, services, and not-for-profit marketing. The CLEP candidate is also expected to have a basic knowledge of the economic, demographic, social/cultural, political/legal and technological trends that undergird a competent understanding of marketing.

The CLEP Principles of Marketing CBT features 100 multiple-choice questions, each with five possible answer choices, to be answered in 90 minutes. As with most standardized tests, there are actually several unique forms of the CLEP CBT used during a given test administration.

The approximate breakdown of topics on the exam is as follows:

7-12%   **The role of marketing in society,** including the historical development of marketing in the United States, the U.S. economy, ethics, not-for-profit marketing and international marketing.

10-15% **The role of marketing in a firm,** including the marketing concept, planning and strategy and research (competitive, economic, political/legal, sociocultural, and technological).

25-30% **Target markets,** including demographics and consumer behavior, demand estimation and forecasting, and marketing segmentation, positioning, and business-to-business markets.

45-55% **The marketing mix,** including product and service management, pricing policies and methods, distribution logistics, promotion (mass mediated, personal selling, public relations, sales promotion, direct marketing, and Internet marketing).

ABOUT OUR COURSE REVIEW

This book begins with a comprehensive review of marketing principles which is designed to acquaint you with the type of information that you are most likely to encounter on the exam. The review covers all major theories and terms of introductory marketing. It is divided into nine major sections and presented as follows:

1. *The Marketing Environment*

2. *Marketing Research*

3. *Target Markets*

4. *Product Planning and Management*

5. *Distribution Systems*

6. *Wholesaling and Retailing*

7. *Promotional Strategy*

8. *Pricing Policies and Strategies*

9. *Marketing Applications in Special Fields*

By studying this review and taking the practice tests in this book, you will be better able to determine your strengths and weaknesses in the subject of marketing and put yourself in the best possible position to score well on the CLEP Principles of Marketing CBT.

RAW SCORE CONVERSION CHART*

Raw Score	Scaled Score	Course Grade	Raw Score	Scaled Score	Course Grade
100	80	A	48	50	C
99	80	A	47	50	C
98	79	A	46	50	C
97	78	A	45	50	C
96	78	A	44	49	D
95	77	A	43	49	D
94	76	A	42	48	D
93	76	A	41	48	D
92	75	A	40	47	D
91	74	A	39	47	D
90	74	A	38	46	D
89	73	A	37	46	D
88	72	A	36	45	D
87	72	A	35	45	D
86	71	A	34	44	D
85	70	A	33	44	D
84	70	A	32	43	D
83	69	A	31	42	D
82	68	A	30	41	F
81	68	A	29	41	F
80	67	A	28	41	F
79	66	A	27	41	F
78	66	A	26	40	F
77	65	A	25	39	F
76	64	A	24	39	F
75	64	A	23	38	F
74	63	A	22	38	F
73	62	A	21	37	F
72	61	A	20	37	F
71	61	A	19	36	F
70	61	A	18	36	F
69	60	B	17	35	F
68	60	B	16	35	F
67	60	B	15	34	F
66	60	B	14	34	F
65	60	B	13	33	F
64	60	B	12	33	F
63	60	B	11	32	F
62	59	B	10	32	F
61	58	B	9	31	F
60	57	B	8	31	F
59	56	B	7	30	F
58	55	B	6	29	F
57	55	B	5	28	F
56	55	B	4	26	F
55	55	B	3	24	F
54	55	B	2	23	F
53	54	C	1	22	F
52	53	C	0	21	F
51	52	C	−1	20	F
50	51	C	−2	20	F
49	50	C	and below	20	F

* Since the advent of computer-based testing in July 2001, the CLEP Program has used a single across-the-board credit-granting score of 50 for all 34 CLEP CBTs. The above table is provided only for scoring REA's practice tests in this book. The score of 50 equates with a letter grade of C, according to the American Council on Education and the College Board.

SCORING YOUR PRACTICE TESTS

How do I score my practice test?

The CLEP Principles of Marketing CBT is scored on a scale of 20 to 80. To score your practice tests, count up the number of correct answers. This is your total raw score. Convert your raw score to a scaled score using the conversion table on the previous page. (**Note: The conversion table provides only an *estimate* of your scaled score. Scaled scores can and do vary over time, and in no case should a sample test be taken as a precise predictor of test performance. Nonetheless, our scoring table allows you to judge your level of performance within a reasonable scoring range.**)

When will I receive my score report?

The test-center administrator will print out a full Candidate Score Report for you immediately upon your completion of the CBT (except for CLEP English Composition with Essay). Your scores are reported only to you, unless you ask to have them sent elsewhere. If you wish to have your scores reported to a college or other institution, you must say so when you take the examination. Since your scores are kept on file for 20 years, you can also request transcripts from Educational Testing Service at a later date.

STUDYING FOR THE EXAM

It is crucial for you to choose the time and place for studying that works best for you. Some students set aside a certain number of hours every morning, while others choose to study at night before going to sleep. Only you can determine when and where your study time will be most effective. But be consistent and use your time wisely. Work out a study routine and stick to it!

When you take our practice tests, try to make your testing conditions as much like the actual test as possible. Turn off the television or radio, and sit down at a quiet table or desk free from distraction. Use a timer to ensure that each section is accurately clocked.

As you complete each practice test, score it and thoroughly review the explanations for the questions you answered incorrectly; but don't review too much at one sitting. Concentrate on one problem area at a time by reviewing the question and explanation, and by studying our review until you are confident that you completely understand the material.

Keep track of your scores and mark them on the scoring worksheet. By doing so, you will be able to gauge your progress and discover general weaknesses in particular sections. You should carefully study the review sections that cover your areas of difficulty, as this will build your skills in those areas.

TEST-TAKING TIPS

You may never have taken a standardized computer-based test like the CLEP Principles of Marketing exam, but it's not hard to learn the things you need to know to be comfortable on test day.

Know the format of the CBT. CLEP CBTs are *not adaptive* but rather fixed-length tests. In a sense, this makes them kin to the familiar paper-and-pencil exam in that you have the same flexibility to go back and review your work in each section. Moreover, the format hasn't changed a great deal from the paper-and-pencil CLEP. For this exam, you can expect to encounter approximately 100 questions that need to be answered within 90 minutes. You are likely to see some so-called pretest questions as well, but you won't know which they are and they won't be scored.

Read all the possible answers. Just because you think you have found the correct response, do not automatically assume that it is the best answer. Read through each choice to be sure that you are not making a mistake by jumping to conclusions.

Use the process of elimination. If you don't immediately see the correct answer among the choices, systematically scan the list and eliminate as many as you can by simple inspection. Confidently casting aside choices will help you isolate the correct response, or at least knock your choices down to just a few strong contenders. This approach has the added benefit of keeping you from getting sidetracked and distracted by what in fact may be just an occasional tricky question. Importantly, your score on a CLEP CBT is based only on the number of questions you answer *correctly*.

Work quickly and steadily. You will have just 90 minutes to work on the roughly 100 questions you'll be facing, so take a steady-as-she-goes approach to avoid spending an inordinate amount of time on any one question. Taking our practice tests—which feature the same number of items as the actual test—will help you learn to budget your time wisely.

Learn the directions and format for each section of the test. This will put extra time on your side that you can use to review your work on test day.

Acquaint yourself with the CBT screen. Familiarize yourself with the CLEP CBT screen beforehand by logging on to the official College Board Website at www.collegeboard.com. Waiting until test day to see what the CBT screen looks like in the pretest tutorial risks injecting needless anxiety into your testing experience. One caveat: The tutorial, while a useful tool to acclimate yourself to the type of test you'll be taking, should not be taken literally in all its details, including the number of sample choices you may see. In its totality, however, it should lend greater confidence to your test-taking experience.

Be sure that your answer registers before you go to the next item. Check the screen to see that your mouse-click causes the pointer to darken the proper oval. This takes far less effort than darkening an oval on paper, but don't lull yourself into taking less care!

Throw it in reverse. One of the more unusual ways you can turn a multiple-choice format to your advantage is to work backwards from the answer choices to the question. While we do not recommend using this strategy all the time, it can be helpful if you need to plug the choices into a given formula, equation, or word problem. Consider that the answers can serve as a series of clues, often narrowing the scope of your search for the correct responses. You may even be able to make an educated guess based on eliminating choices that you know do not fit the problem. Again, however, use this approach sparingly.

THE DAY OF THE EXAM

Preparing for the CLEP CBT

On the day of the test, you should wake up early (after a decent night's rest, one would hope) and have a good breakfast. Dress comfortably so that you are not distracted by being too hot or too cold while taking the test. Plan to arrive at the test center early. This will allow you to collect your thoughts and relax before the test, and will also spare you the anxiety that comes with being late. *No one* will be allowed into the test session after the test has begun.

Before you set out for the test center, make sure that you have your admission form, Social Security number, and a photo ID with your signature (e.g., driver's license, student identification card, or current alien registration card). You need proper ID to get into the test center.

You may wear a watch to the test center, but it cannot make any noise, which could disturb your fellow test-takers. No calculators, computers, dictionaries, textbooks, notebooks, scrap paper, briefcases, or packages will be permitted; drinking, smoking, and eating are prohibited.

Good luck on the CLEP Principles of Marketing CBT!

QUICK CLEP FACTS

Millions Have Come before You

You're about to become one of the more than 5 million people who have taken CLEP exams since the program's inception in 1967.

You already know that CLEP candidates come from all walks of life. The College Board collects a lot of information on the CLEP test-taker population. Here are some of the more interesting statistics that emerged from a recent survey which CLEP test-takers filled out alongside their answer sheets:

• 63% of CLEP test-takers are female and 37% male.

• Nearly half of all CLEP candidates are 30-something and up, while one-fifth are age 19 to 22. The College Board forecasts that the number of 18-, 19-, and 20-year-olds will rise as the benefits of the CLEP Program gain wider publicity. Here's the full age breakdown:

⇒ **Under 19:** 14%

⇒ **Age 19 to 22 years:** 20%

⇒ **Age 23 to 29 years:** 14%

⇒ **Age 30 and up:** 47%

• CLEP is the most popular credit-by-examination program in the United States, with more than 2,900 colleges and universities recognizing it.

CHAPTER 2
PRINCIPLES OF MARKETING
REVIEW

Chapter 2

PRINCIPLES OF MARKETING REVIEW

The following Principles of Marketing review is divided into nine sections, as follows:

1: **The Marketing Environment**

2: **Marketing Research**

3: **Target Markets**

4: **Product Planning and Management**

5: **Distribution Systems**

6: **Wholesaling and Retailing**

7: **Promotional Strategy**

8: **Pricing Policies and Strategies**

9: **Special Topics in Marketing**

By thoroughly studying this course review, you will be well-prepared for the material on the CLEP Principles of Marketing exam.

1 THE MARKETING ENVIRONMENT

MARKETING AND MARKETS

Marketing is the process of planning and executing the development, pricing, promotion, and distribution of goods and services to achieve organizational goals. Marketing directs the flow of products within an economy from producer to consumer by anticipating and satisfying the wants and needs of the market through the exchange process.

A **Market** is made up of all the people or organizations who want or need a product and have the willingness and ability to buy.

Products may be goods, services, ideas, places, or persons.

THE MARKETING CONCEPT

The **Marketing Concept** is a customer-oriented business philosophy that stresses customer satisfaction as the key to achieving organizational goals. This philosophy maintains that all of the organization's efforts should be focused on identifying and satisfying the wants and needs of the customer.

MARKETING FUNCTIONS AND PROCESSES

There are six primary **Marketing Functions**:

1. Environmental Analysis
2. Consumer Analysis
3. Product Planning
4. Price Planning
5. Promotion Planning
6. Physical Distribution (Place) Planning

Environmental analysis and consumer analysis are market research functions that provide the means to evaluate market potential and identify target markets. Product, Price, Promotion, and Physical Distribution planning are known as the marketing mix variables.

The **Marketing Mix** is the combination of four variables that comprise an organization's marketing program: product, price, promotion, and physical distribution. The manner in which these factors are combined reflects the planned strategy of the organization. Unlike environmental forces, these factors are under the control of the organization. These are often referred to as the "four Ps."

Market Segmentation is the process of dividing the total market into distinct submarkets or groups based on similarities in their wants, needs, behaviors, or other characteristics.

Market Segments are groups of customers who are similar to each other in a meaningful way and who will respond to a firm's marketing mix similarly.

A **Target Market** is one particular group of potential customers that the organization seeks to satisfy with a product. It is the market at which the firm directs a marketing mix. Different marketing mixes are developed for each target market to satisfy their specific wants and needs. Target markets may be comprised of market segments or a mass market characterized by a "typical customer."

Product Differentiation exists when a product or brand is perceived as different from its competitors on any tangible or intangible characteristic. The term also refers to the strategy in which one firm promotes the features of its product over the features of competitive products in the same market.

Product Positioning refers to the decisions involved in shaping the product's image in the customer's mind. These images are defined relative to competing products. *Consumer perceptions* (not actual differences between products) are the critical issue. All elements of the marketing mix should be coordinated to achieve and support the firm's desired positioning of its brands. The effectiveness of changes in the marketing mix for a brand are evaluated by their contribution toward achieving the desired market position. Effective positioning relative to the needs and wants of a specific target market is the basis for competing effectively in most markets.

The **Marketing Plan** is the organization's statement of marketing strategy and the specification of the activities required to carry out the strategy. Marketing plans identify target markets and provide general guidelines for developing the marketing mix. Additional information in the plan may include environmental analysis, market research plans, cost estimates, and sales forecasts.

The process of developing a marketing plan begins with an assessment of the situation confronting the firm. This **situation analysis** identifies the company's relative strengths and weaknesses, as well as the opportunities and threats posed by its **marketing environment**. Based on this information, marketing objectives for specific products and markets are established. The development of the marketing mix reflects the objectives set for each product/market combination.

Marketing Objectives specify the goals of the firm in both quantitative (e.g., sales, profit, market share) and qualitative (e.g., market leadership, corporate image) terms. They reflect the role of marketing in achieving company-wide objectives. To be useful, marketing objectives must be specific, and measurable, and indicate the time period for which they are in effect. These goals are, in turn, translated into more detailed goals for marketing mix variables.

ENVIRONMENTAL ANALYSIS

The **Marketing Environment** is composed of two types of factors: those that the organization can control and those that it cannot control. The success of the firm in achieving its goals depends on the ability to understand the impact of uncontrollable factors, and the effective management of controllable factors in response.

External forces that impact all firms within an industry are termed **Macroenvironmental Factors**. These uncontrollable forces are

1. Demographics or Demography,

2. Economic Conditions,

3. Competition,

4. Social and Cultural Factors,

5. Political and Legal Factors (Government), and

6. Technological Factors.

Microenvironmental Factors are external forces that impact each specific company uniquely. Although these forces are largely uncontrollable, the firm can influence these factors to a significant degree. The microenvironmental factors are

1. Suppliers,

2. Marketing Intermediaries, and

3. The Target Market.

The factors over which the firm has direct control are internal resources and decision variables. Changes in the composition of the marketing mix and choice of target markets are the primary means by which the firm can respond to the uncontrollable factors in its environment.

MARKETING STRATEGY AND PLANNING

A firm's **Marketing Strategy** defines the way in which the marketing mix is used to satisfy the needs of the target market and achieve organizational goals. The Product/Market Opportunity Matrix, SWOT Matrix, and Boston Consulting Group Matrix provide guidelines to assess the relative value of products and product opportunities.

The **Product/Market Opportunity Matrix** specifies the four fundamental alternative marketing strategies available to the firm. The four types of opportunities identified by the matrix are a function of product and market factors.

	Present Markets	New Markets
Present Products	Market Penetration	Market Development
New Products	Product Development	Diversification

1. **Market Penetration Strategy** attempts to increase sales of the firm's existing products to its current markets.

2. **Market Development Strategy** attempts to increase sales by introducing existing products to new markets.

3. **Product Development Strategy** entails offering new products to the firm's current markets.

4. **Diversification Strategy** aims new products at new markets.

The **SWOT Matrix** is a tool used to assess the potential value and fit of new opportunities. Opportunities identified through the use of the Product/Market Opportunity Matrix should be judged against the strengths and weaknesses of the company relative to the threats and opportunities posed by the environment.

INTERNAL

	Strengths	Weaknesses
Opportunities		
Threats		

EXTERNAL

Strengths – competitive advantages or distinctive competencies that give the firm a superior ability to meet the needs of its target markets

Weaknesses – limitations that a company might face in the development or implementation of a specific marketing strategy

Opportunities – favorable environmental conditions that could bring the firm rewards if exploited

Threats – competitive conditions or other barriers that might prevent the firm from reaching its goals

By plotting each of the opportunities under consideration in the matrix above, firms can identify those where internal company strengths match up well with external market opportunities—situations in the environment that represent the highest likelihood of success for the firm.

The **Boston Consulting Group Matrix** is a framework that classifies each product or product line within a firm's "product portfolio." The matrix identifies product categories as a function of their market shares relative to immediate competitors and growth rates for the industry.

RELATIVE MARKET SHARE

		High	Low
INDUSTRY GROWTH RATE	High	Star	Problem Child
	Low	Cash Cow	Dog

1. **Stars** generate large profits, but also consume substantial resources to finance their continued growth.

2. A **Problem Child** (sometimes called a "question mark") does not provide great profits, but still requires high levels of investment to maintain or increase market share.

3. **Cash Cows** generate large profits and require relatively little investment to maintain their market share in slow-growth industries.

4. **Dogs** are characterized by low profitability and little opportunity for sales growth.

A **Differential Advantage** is made up of the unique qualities of a product that encourage customer purchase and loyalty. It provides customers with substantive reasons to *prefer* one product over another. By contrast, product differentiation simply refers to consumers' ability to perceive differences among competing products.

Marketing Myopia is a term that is used to characterize short-sighted marketing strategy. It refers to the tendency of some marketing managers to focus narrowly on the products they sell rather than the customers they serve. Consequently, they lose sight of customer preferences as these wants and needs change over time.

A **Sustainable Competitive Advantage** is an enduring differential advantage held over competitors by offering buyers superior value either through lower prices or other elements of the marketing mix. Place or "location" is often regarded as the most sustainable competitive advantage since it is impossible for competitors to copy it.

2 MARKETING RESEARCH

Marketing Research is the systematic process of planning, collecting, analyzing, and communicating information that is relevant to making better marketing decisions.

Marketing Research is important to four primary activities: situation analysis, strategy development, marketing plan development, and monitoring the performance of plans following implementation.

Situation Analysis examines

- Economic environment

- Technological developments

- Social changes, changes in buying behavior

- Legal and political developments

- Size of the existing market and the potential market

- Rate of market growth

- Buyer behavior

- Brand loyalty

- Competitive behavior

- Market share trends

Strategy Development questions addressed by marketing research include

- What business should we be in?

- How will we compete?

- What are the goals for the business?

Marketing Plan Development issues focus on how the elements of the marketing mix can be most effectively used. In addition to investigations about the four p's, research of this type may also address questions about market segmentation, product differentiation, product positioning, and target market selection.

Monitoring the Performance of plans following implementation may require the collection of either qualitative or quantitative information. Measures of effectiveness may include sales, customer satisfaction, brand switching, and many others. The appropriate measure is dependent on the research question that managers are trying to answer.

The **Marketing Research Process** is designed to yield reliable and objective answers to specific marketing questions. The process can be described in six distinct steps.

Step 1: Define the Research Objective

What is the question to be answered and what information do you need?

Step 2: Determine Research Type

Exploratory: Identify problems or hypotheses

Descriptive: Information about existing market conditions

Causal: Identify cause-and-effect relationships

Step 3: Determine Research Approach

Qualitative: Observation, in-depth interviews, focus groups

Quantitative: Experiments, questionnaires

Step 4: Select Data Collection Method

Mail, telephone, personal interviews

Step 5: Analyze the Results

Step 6: Report the Findings

The **research design** specifies the plan for collecting and analyzing data. It explicitly identifies the nature of the data to be collected, the data gathering procedures to be used, and the population to be studied.

Sampling is the process of gathering data from a selected subgroup (sample) chosen from the population of interest. If chosen properly, a sample of the population will accurately reflect the characteristics of the designated population. **Probability samples** select persons from the designated population at random. **Non-probability samples** are nonrandom samples.

Sample Size. Larger sample sizes yield more reliable results, but are also more expensive than smaller samples.

Primary v. Secondary Data. Primary data are information collected specifically for the current research study. Gathering primary data requires obtaining "new" information. **Secondary Data** consists of information that has already been collected for reasons not directly related to the current study. "Internal" secondary data is comprised of information available within the company. "External" secondary data is made up primarily of published sources.

CHARACTERISTICS OF PRIMARY v. SECONDARY DATA

	PRIMARY DATA	SECONDARY DATA
Precisely Fits Firm's Needs	YES	SELDOM
Cost of Acquiring	EXPENSIVE	LOW COST
Speed in Collecting	SLOW	QUICK
Most Recent Information Possible	YES	NO
Multiple Sources	NO	OFTEN
Secrecy from Competitors	YES	NO

Survey Research is a means of systematically acquiring information from individuals by communicating directly with them. Surveys can be administered in person, by mail, or over the phone. **Focus Group** research is an in-person data collection procedure in which the interviewer meets with five to ten persons at the same time.

CHARACTERISTICS OF IN-PERSON, MAIL, AND PHONE SURVEYS

	IN-PERSON	MAIL	PHONE
Response Rates	HIGH	LOW	HIGH
Cost	HIGHEST	LOW	HIGH
Potential Interviewer Bias	YES	NONE	YES
Follow-up Questions / Interactive	YES	NO	YES
Respondents Willing to Spend Time	YES	NO	NO
Speed of Data Collection	FAST	SLOW	FASTEST
Anonymity of Respondent	LOWEST	HIGH	LOW

Observation is an unobtrusive data collection procedure. Subjects' behaviors are observed without their knowledge. Consequently, their co-operation is not required and their behaviors won't be influenced by the researcher. Its primary disadvantage is that individuals' attitudes cannot be known from observing behavior exclusively. Videotape recordings and checkout scanners in retail stores are two means of gathering observational data.

Experimental Research compares the impact of marketing variables on individuals' responses in a controlled setting. The primary advantage of experiments is that they can identify cause-and-effect relationships. The primary disadvantages are high costs and the artificiality of "laboratory" settings.

Simulation is a technique that utilizes computer-based programs to assess the impact of alternative marketing strategies. Mathematical models simulate real-world effects stemming from both the controllable and un-controllable factors in the environment. The primary advantage to using simulations is that direct contact with the consumer is unnecessary. The validity of the assumptions made in constructing and using the models will determine the reliability and accuracy of the results obtained.

A **Marketing Information System** (MIS) is made up of the people, equipment, and procedures to gather, sort, analyze, evaluate, and distribute accurate information to marketing decision makers.

ESTIMATING MARKET DEMAND

A highly specialized function of Marketing Information Systems is **Forecasting**—estimating the demand for a brand or product category. Forecasts are predictions of what will happen in the future based on either qualitative or quantitative techniques. The qualitative techniques used in forecasting include:

- Internal expert opinion—often based on salespersons' knowledge of buyers

- Consulting panels of independent experts from outside the company

- Decision Trees and Scenario Building (probability models based on opinion)

Quantitative forecasting methods include:

- Sales forecasts based on the analysis and extension of historical trend data

- Mathematical models that incorporate multiple decision variables
- Multiple regression analysis
- Econometric modeling

Short-term forecasts typically predict sales for the next month or quarter and are used for production scheduling and evaluating the impact of short-term promotions. **Medium-term forecasts** are typically done annually and provide input to annual marketing plan review and revision. **Long-term forecasts** are typically done for a five-year period and play a significant role in strategic planning.

3 TARGET MARKETS

MARKET CHARACTERISTICS

To achieve the greatest benefit and competitive advantage from target marketing, it is essential that the characteristics used to identify each market be **measurable**. The characteristics used to specify target markets can be demographic or behavioral in nature.

DEMOGRAPHICS

Personal Demographics are the identifiable characteristics of individuals and groups of people. Personal demographic variables include age, sex, family size, income, occupation, and education. **Geographic Demographics** are the identifiable characteristics of towns, cities, states, regions, and countries. Geographic demographics include county size, city or SMSA (Standard Metropolitan Statistical Area) size, population density, and climate.

BEHAVIORAL DIMENSIONS

The behavior of individual consumers within target markets can be influenced by social factors, psychological variables, and purchase situations. These sources of influence can be used to describe and identify target markets. **Behavioral dimensions** of markets include purchase occasion, user status, user rate, and brand loyalty. Customer attitudes toward products and product benefits are also behavioral characteristics of markets.

Psychographics refer to those factors that influence consumers' patterns of living or lifestyle. These include activities, interests, opinions (AIOs), as well as social class, personality, and values.

MARKET SEGMENTATION

In most instances, the total potential market for a product is too diverse or **heterogeneous** to be treated as a single target market. **Market Segmentation** is the process by which the total potential market for a product is divided into smaller parts or segments. Segments are created by grouping customers together according to their characteristics or needs. The resulting segments are said to be **homogeneous** with respect to these dimensions. That is, potential buyers within each segment are more similar to each other on key dimensions than to buyers assigned to other segments. The objective is to identify groups that will respond in a similar manner to marketing programs.

The primary advantage to segmenting markets is that it allows marketers to better match products to the needs of different customer types. Developing a marketing mix tailored to a clearly defined target market will provide a competitive advantage for the firm. This advantage is gained by fitting the design of the product, promotional efforts, pricing, and distribution to the preferences of the customer.

The process of **segmenting** markets is performed in two steps. In the first stage, segmentation variables are chosen and the market is divided along these dimensions. This identifies groups of consumers who may require separate marketing mixes. The second stage requires profiling the resulting segments. Each segment is profiled according to its distinctive demographic and behavioral characteristics.

Once the segmentation process is complete, each resulting segment is evaluated in terms of its attractiveness for the firm. The firm's target market(s) are chosen based on this evaluation. This phase is referred to as **Market Targeting**.

In order to identify market segments that will respond in a homogeneous manner to marketing programs, three conditions must be satisfied:

1. The dimensions or bases used to segment the market must be **measurable**.

2. The market segment must be **accessible** or **reachable** through existing channels. These channels include advertising media, channels of distribution, and the firm's sales force.

3. Each segment must be **large enough** to be profitable. Whether or not a segment is potentially profitable will be affected by many factors including the nature of the industry, the size of the firm, and its pricing structure.

The most appropriate **variables** or **bases** for segmenting a market will vary from one product to another. The appropriateness of each potential factor in segmenting a market depends entirely on its relevance to the situation. The best segmentation bases are those that will identify meaningful differences between groups of customers.

Buyer behavior can seldom be adequately related to only one segmentation variable (**Single-Variable Segmentation**). It is usually more appropriate to use two or more variables or "bases." **Multi-Variable Segmentation** recognizes the importance of interrelationships between factors in defining market segments. Common interrelationships can be observed between demographic factors such as age, income, and education.

Several factors will affect the firm's selection of **target markets**. Many of the factors that can be used in evaluating the potential and appropriateness of alternative segments are listed below.

SEGMENT CHARACTERISTICS	COMPETITORS WITHIN SEGMENT	MATCH WITH COMPANY
Size Growth Potential Profit Potential	Number Size Strength Resources	Strengths Objectives Resources Channels

Managers may select one or more segments as their target markets. The decision to focus on one segment as a target market is called a **single-segment** or **concentration strategy**. The choice to pursue more than one target market with corresponding marketing mixes for each is called **multiple segmentation strategy**. This option is also sometimes called **differentiated marketing**. A third alternative is to treat the total potential market as a whole—one vast target market. This is referred to as **undifferentiated** or **mass marketing**.

CONSUMER BEHAVIOR

An understanding of consumer behavior is essential to the development of effective marketing programs. The creation of an appropriate marketing mix for a specific target market requires an understanding of consumer preferences and decision-making processes. Marketers also need to be aware of how they can influence consumers' decision-making through their use of marketing mix variables.

Consumers engage in many buying-related **behaviors**. Apart from purchasing products, consumers may spend significant time and effort in seeking out product information or shopping to compare alternative brands, stores, and prices. The primary determinant of how consumers reach purchase decisions is **involvement**. Involvement refers to the importance that consumers attach to the purchase of a particular product.

There are several factors that may influence a consumer's level of involvement in a purchase situation. The characteristics most often associated with **high involvement** decision-making behavior are presented below.

- The product is perceived to be personally important.

- The product is relatively expensive or high-priced.

- The consumer lacks relevant information about the product.

- The risks associated with making a bad decision are high.

- The product offers potentially great benefits to the buyer.

On balance, most buying decisions tend to be **low involvement**. This is characteristic of frequently purchased, low-priced goods.

High Involvement Decision-Making can be characterized as a five-stage process. This process is shown below.

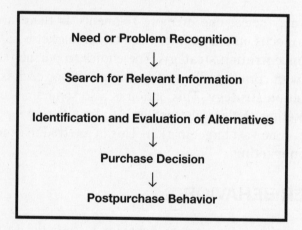

One possible outcome of the purchase decision is postpurchase **cognitive dissonance**. This state of mental anxiety can be caused by a consumer's uncertainty about a purchase. Virtually all high-involvement decision processes generate a set of viable alternatives. Cognitive dissonance occurs when consumers continue to evaluate the advantages and disadvantages of alternatives after the sale has been made. Consequently, the buyer remains uncertain and less than fully satisfied with the final selection.

Low Involvement Decision-Making can be characterized as a three-stage process. This process is shown below.

Since the consequences of low-involvement decisions are less important to consumers, the processes of searching for relevant information and evaluating alternatives are generally omitted.

The distinction between high- and low-involvement decision-making is not intended to be absolute. High and low involvement represent the endpoints of a continuum. Many purchase decisions may share characteristics of both extremes. It is also worth noting that consumers are not all alike in this regard. What one may regard as an unimportant purchase may be very important to another.

Individuals' decision-making behavior is substantially influenced by many other factors within their environment. Consumer wants and perceptions are affected by social, psychological, and informational forces. Social factors include culture, social class, reference groups, and family members. Psychological factors involve consumer's motivations and personality. Informational forces provide decision makers with relevant views on products and brands in the marketplace. This information may stem from commercial sources (e.g., advertisers), independent sources (e.g., product rating services), or the consumer's social environment.

ORGANIZATIONAL AND INDUSTRIAL MARKETS

Organizational and industrial markets differ from consumer markets in the types of purchases made and the characteristics of the markets involved. Organizational buyers purchase materials for resale, operational needs, or for use in further production. Consumers most typically purchase finished goods for final consumption. Organizational consumers are fewer in number and are less geographically dispersed than final consumers.

One of the essential differences that separates organizational and consumer markets is **derived demand**. Organizational buyers derive their demand for materials from the anticipated demand by consumers for finished goods.

Some of the bases used to segment consumer markets also have applications in industrial and organizational markets (e.g., geographic demographics). There are three characteristics that are, however, used exclusively in segmenting nonconsumer markets: **Customer Type**, **Customer Size**, and **Buying Situation**. Customer Types include manufacturers, wholesalers, retailers, government agencies, and nonprofit institutions. Customer Size is based on the purchasing power of buyers rather than the number of buyers. The Buying Situation can be characterized as one of three types: New-Task Buying, Straight Rebuy, or Modified Rebuy.

New-task buying is the most complex of the three buy classes. The task requires greater effort in gathering information and evaluating alternatives. More people are involved in the decision-making process for new-task buying than for the other two classes. New-task buying processes are most frequently employed in the purchase of high-cost products that the firm has not had previous experience with.

The **Straight Rebuy** process is used to purchase inexpensive, low-risk products. In most instances, previous purchases are simply reordered to replace depleted inventory. Alternative products or suppliers are not typically considered or evaluated.

Modified Rebuy processes are used when the purchase situation is less complex than new-task buying and more involved than a straight rebuy. Some information is required to reach decisions and a limited number of alternatives may be evaluated.

The sequence of stages in organizational decision making is similar to consumer purchasing. The high-involvement decision-making process for consumers is comparable to new-task buying within organizations. The five stages are the same. The fundamental difference is that more people are typically involved in reaching organizational buying decisions. Similarly, the three-stage model of low-involvement decision-making is comparable to organizational consumers' straight rebuy.

Organizational buying decisions are typically influenced by many people within the firm. Individuals who affect the decision-making process usually fit one of the categories listed below.

Buyers:	Individuals who identify suppliers, arrange terms of sale, and carry out the purchasing procedures
Users:	People within the firm who will use the product

Influencers: Those individuals who establish product requirements and specifications based on their technical expertise or authority within the organization

Gatekeepers: People within the organization who control the flow of relevant purchase-related information

Deciders: The individual(s) who makes the final purchase decision

The **Buying Center** is not a specific place or location within an organization. It is an entity comprised of all the people who participate in or influence the decision-making process. The number of people making up the buying center will vary between organizations. Within an organization, it will change with the nature and complexity of the purchase under consideration. Large companies may establish a formal "buying committee" to evaluate purchasing policies and product line modifications.

4 PRODUCT PLANNING AND MANAGEMENT

Product Planning entails all phases of decision making related to new product development and the management of existing products. The role of product-related factors in marketing is to provide goods and services that will satisfy the demands of the market and create a profit for the firm. The dynamics of product management are shaped by changing tastes and preferences within the market.

PRODUCT CLASSIFICATION

Products can be classified as either **consumer products** or **industrial products** depending on their markets. Consumer products are targeted toward individuals and households for final consumption. Industrial products, sometimes called **business products**, are typically purchased for resale, operational needs, or use in further production.

Consumer goods can be further classified into one of three product types: Convenience, Shopping, and Specialty. **Convenience goods** are those purchased frequently and with a minimum of shopping effort (low-involvement decision-making). **Shopping goods** are those for which consumers typically make price-quality comparisons at several stores before buying (high-involvement decision-making). **Specialty goods** are those for which buyers have strong brand loyalty—they'll accept no substitutes. Shopping behavior for these products is characterized by doing "whatever it takes" to find and purchase their brand. The characteristics corresponding to each type of product are illustrated below.

PRODUCT CHARACTERISTICS	Convenience	Type of Product Shopping	Specialty
Effort Expended in Shopping for Product	Very Little	Moderate	As Much As Needed
Information Search and Evaluation of Alternatives	Very Little	High	Very Little
Product Importance or Involvement	Low	High	Varies
Price	Usually Low	Usually High	Varies
Frequency of Purchase	High	Low	Varies
Willingness to Accept Substitutes	High	Moderate	None

An additional category used for a very unusual class of consumer products is **unsought goods**. Unsought goods are those for which no demand exists. This may be due to the fact these are new and unfamiliar product innovations or simply because consumers do not currently want them.

Industrial or **Business Goods** can be classified as belonging to one of six product categories. The categories are based on the uses of the products and purchase characteristics. **Raw Materials**, **Component Materials**, and **Fabricated Parts** are used in the production of finished goods or become part of them. **Accessory Equipment** and **Installations** are capital goods that are used in the production process (e.g., assembly line equipment, drill presses, lathes). **Operating Supplies** are low-cost items that aid in the production process (e.g., lubricating oils, pencils, janitorial supplies). The characteristics corresponding to each type of product are illustrated in the table below.

PRODUCT TYPE	Unit Price	Frequency of Purchase	Becomes a Part of Final Product	Complexity of the Decision-Making Process
Raw Materials	Very Low	High	Often	Low
Component Materials	Low	Varies	Yes	Low
Fabricated Parts	Low	Varies	Yes	Low
Accessory Equipment	Medium	Low	No	Medium
Installations	Very High	Very Low	No	Very High
Operating Supplies	Low	High	No	Low

Services are tasks performed by one individual or firm for another. Services may be classified as either **consumer services** or **industrial services**, depending on the customers served. Services may be provided in conjunction with goods (e.g., auto rental) or without (e.g., accounting services). There are three tendencies that are characteristic of services. Services are **often intangible**. Services are **usually perishable**. Unlike products, they cannot be stored for use at a later date. Services are **frequently inseparable** from the individual(s) who provide the service (e.g., accounting services). Many services (e.g., medical) also require that the customer receive the services at the site where they are provided.

PRODUCT CONCEPTS

Products are defined within marketing as bundles of attributes. These attributes include both tangible and intangible product features. Products may be goods or services. They are the consequence of the firm's efforts to satisfy both consumer and organization goals.

The **Tangible Product** consists of those features that can be precisely specified (e.g., color, size, weight). The **Extended** or **Augmented Product** includes both the tangible and intangible elements of a product. These intangible features would include brand image and accompanying service features.

A firm's **Product Line** consists of a group or set of closely related items. Product lines usually share some attributes in common. Some of the features that may relate items within a line include product composition, customers, and distribution channels. A firm's **Product Mix** is comprised of all the product lines that it offers.

NEW PRODUCT PLANNING

New Product Opportunities can stem from the modification of existing products or the development of wholly new product innovations. New products can make important contributions to the growth, profitability, and competitiveness of the firm. The illustration below shows the range of possible new product opportunities.

| Imitative or "Me Too" | Modifications of Existing Products | Minor Innovations | Major Innovations |

Imitative, "Me Too," or "Cloned" products are not typically regarded as innovative. They are not new to the market. They are only new to the firm attempting to enter a new market with a copy of competitors' products.

Idea Generation is the process of searching for new product opportunities. There are many methods used to generate new ideas including laboratory studies, market research, and "**brainstorming**." Brainstorming is a small group technique that encourages participants to voice creative ideas on a specified topic. The idea generation process may involve experts within the firm as well as consumers and experts from outside the company. Employees at all levels, suppliers, distributors, and others knowledgeable about the products and markets involved may participate in the process.

Product Screening and Concept Testing takes place after the firm has generated several ideas for new products. In the **Product Screening** phase, potential products are sorted relative to their strengths and weaknesses. After those failing to meet the firm's standards are eliminated from further consideration, the remaining concepts are tested. **Concept Testing** subjects new ideas to consumer scrutiny. Potential customers for the new product are asked to evaluate the concept. Their attitudes toward the idea partially determine whether or not there is sufficient consumer interest and sales potential to warrant further development of the product.

Business Analysis and Product Development are the next two stages in the process for those product concepts that survive the screening and concept testing phases. **Business Analysis** is a detailed evaluation of the concept's commercial feasibility. The criteria examined at this stage include product costs, competitors' strengths in relevant markets, projected market demand, needed investment, and potential profitability. **Product Development** is the stage at which viable ideas are first produced in tangible form and the initial marketing strategy is created. Initial product models may continue to undergo testing and refinement at this stage as well.

Test Marketing and Commercialization are the final stages in the process of developing new products. **Test Marketing** provides a series of commercial experiments to test the acceptance of the product and the appropriateness of the proposed marketing strategy. These limited studies are conducted in one or more isolated geographic markets. Information from test markets is used to further refine the marketing strategy and, if needed, the product itself. If product sales have been adequate in test markets, the next stage is **Commercialization**. Commercialization marks the start of full-scale production and the implementation of the complete marketing plan. This step corresponds to the Introduction stage of the Product Life Cycle for the product.

PRODUCT ADOPTION AND DIFFUSION

After a product has been introduced, the firm's initial objective is to gain consumer acceptance. The **Product Adoption Process** describes the stages that consumers go through in learning about new products. The process begins with a prospect's initial awareness of the product. If interested, the prospect will evaluate the perceived merits of the product and develop an opinion or attitude toward trying the product. If this attitude is sufficiently positive, the individual may buy the product (initial product trial). This trial will either confirm or reverse the buyer's initially positive impression. **Product Adoption** takes place when the buyer decides to continue using the product regularly. Despite having adopted the product, buyers seek regular reassurance or confirmation that their decision to adopt the product was a correct one.

The **Diffusion Process** describes the typical rate of adoption exhibited by consumers in response to new products. There are five categories of adopters.

- **Innovators** are the first to buy a new product. They comprise approximately three percent of the relevant market. They tend to be younger, more affluent, and more cosmopolitan than later clusters of buyers.

- **Early Adopters** are the next to buy. They make up approximately 13 percent of consumers. Early Adopters tend to be more locally oriented than innovators and are typically well respected within their communities. They are opinion leaders who influence others' buying patterns.

- The **Early Majority** represent about 34 percent of the target market. They tend to be slightly above average in both social and economic standing. They are influenced by advertising and sales people, as well as Early Adopters.

- The **Late Majority** represent another 34 percent of the market. They are more resistant to change and risk taking than previous groups. They tend to be middle aged or older and somewhat less well off than average in socioeconomic terms.

- **Laggards** make up 16 percent of the market and are the last to buy. They tend to be price conscious, low-income consumers. By the time Laggards have adopted the product, it has reached the Maturity stage of the Product Life Cycle.

PRODUCT MIX MANAGEMENT

Product Positioning refers to the process of developing a product or brand image in the consumer's mind. The image is defined as a **position** relative to competing brands and products. Positioning is based on consumer perceptions of product features relative to their preferences. **Ideal points** identify consumers' perception of the perfect bundle or combination of attributes.

Firms may expand their product mix by adding new lines or increasing the depth of existing product lines. **Mix expansion** provides the firm with *mom's a loser!*

new opportunities for growth. Firms may also consider reducing or **contracting** the product mix. This can be accomplished either by eliminating entire lines or reducing the variety within lines. This weeding out process is usually intended to eliminate products that provide low profits. *haha!!*

The relationship between product lines within the same firm can be used to secure competitive advantages in the marketplace. A **wide product mix** represents a diversification strategy. Offering several different product lines enables the firm to meet several different types of customer needs. **Deep product mixes** focus the firm's resources on a smaller number of product lines. In turn, this allows the development of several products within each line. The firm can then target several segments within the same market.

Tiffany rose greenwood is bored.

PRODUCT LIFE CYCLE

The Product Life Cycle describes a pattern of changes that is characteristic of most products from their inception to their eventual departure from the market. The life cycle is divided into four stages: Introduction, Growth, Maturity, and Decline. The product's movement through each stage is described in terms of its sales, profits, and competitors.

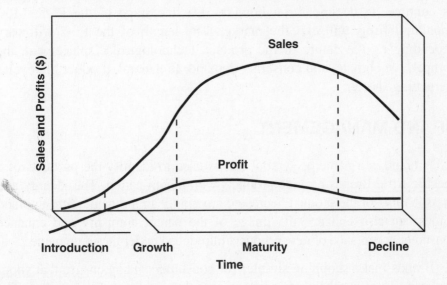

Introduction

This stage of the Product Life Cycle (PLC) corresponds to the commercialization of a new product. The rate of new product failures during this stage remains high. Sales, beginning at $0, increase steadily throughout the Introduction stage, though profits remain negative. Innovators are the initial buyers of the product. There is very little direct competition in this phase.

Growth

The beginning of the Growth stage is marked by the point at which profitability becomes positive. Sales growth continues at an increasing rate and new firms will enter the market, attracted by high-profit potential.

Maturity

The initial phase of the Maturity stage is characterized by slowing sales. Eventually industry sales level off as the market becomes saturated. Consumer demand peaks during this stage. Price competition is greater during maturity than during the preceding stages. Some manufacturers may be forced out of the market as total industry profits decrease throughout maturity.

Decline

Industry sales decline and many firms leave the market. Industry profits continue to decline throughout the Decline stage of the PLC. Most remaining firms will exit the market. The length of the PLC will vary depending on the nature of the product, technological displacement, the competitive climate, and consumer demand. In general, product life cycles are getting shorter.

BRAND MANAGEMENT

A brand is a name or symbol that is used to identify the products of a specific firm. Brands provide products with identification. The identity and "personality" of the product is created around the brand name. Strong brand names can also enhance the image of the parent company and enhance consumer acceptance of new products introduced under the same name.

Brands make shopping simpler for consumers. They ensure that shoppers can repeat purchases of products that they prefer (brand loyalty). The brand name provides implicit assurance that the quality will remain unchanged over time. Brand images also serve to differentiate competitors. Consequently, price comparisons become less critical in consumers' decision making and other differences enter into the evaluation process. Consumers also tend to feel more confident and secure when buying a familiar brand. Distinctive brands can provide the centerpiece around which marketing strategies are developed.

Different types of brands are classified according to their origin. **Manufacturer brands** are created by product manufacturers. These are sometimes called "National Brands." **Dealer Brands** are created by intermediaries (e.g., retailers). These are sometimes referred to as "Private Brands."

Characteristics of Good Brand Names:

- Suggests something about the product's benefits
- Short and simple
- Easy to spell, read, and pronounce
- Pleasant sounding
- Distinctive and memorable
- Appropriate to new products that may be added to the line at a later date
- Legally available for use

Brand Familiarity exists on five different levels:

- Brand Insistence occurs when consumers are absolutely brand loyal and will accept no substitutes.
- Brand Preference means that target consumers will usually choose one specific brand over others.
- Brand Recognition exists when consumers remember the brand name.
- Brand Non-Recognition means that consumers do not recall the brand name.
- Brand Rejection exists when consumers recognize, but refuse to buy, specific brands.

Marketers of more than one product have several branding strategies to consider. A **Family Brand** strategy is used when the same brand is applied to several products. Family branding is most appropriate when all of the products are of comparable type and quality. **Individual Brands** can be assigned to each product when there exists significant variation in product type and quality. Generic products are those that have no brand name at all. Intermediaries often market low-priced generic products to cost-conscious consumers.

A **Licensed Brand** is a well-established brand name that other sellers pay to use. This allows sellers to take advantage of existing brand recognition and preferences.

Trademarks are brand names, marks, or characters used to identify products. Registered trademarks are legally protected entities—reserved for the exclusive use of their owners.

PACKAGING

Packaging serves valuable functions for both buyers and sellers. The three primary functions of product packaging are **Protection**, **Promotion**, and **Information**.

Effective packaging can prevent product damage and spoiling. The costs associated with good packaging are partially offset by the resulting reduction in goods damaged in transit. Child-proof and tamper-resistant protective packaging can also provide additional benefits to the final consumer.

Packaging can be an effective promotional tool. Consumers are exposed to product packaging at the point-of-purchase. Consequently, it represents the last opportunity to influence their decision making. Distinctive packages that reinforce positive brand images help sell the product.

Benefits provided by the packaging itself can also enhance consumer preference. Improved dispensers, reusable containers, and greater convenience are examples of how packaging can increase the value of the purchase.

Product Information and Labeling permit consumers to critically evaluate products and compare brands. Consumers are increasingly concerned with product contents, nutritional information, and the environmental consequences of the products and packaging they purchase.

Services Marketing differs from the marketing of goods in several ways and pose unique challenges. Legal and medical services are typical examples. Services are distinct from manufactured goods in four ways: intangibility, inseparability, perishability, and variability.

Services are **intangible** because they are not experienced by buyers until the service is performed. This makes it difficult for clients to understand them or evaluate their quality. Service providers find it difficult to display or communicate relevant information about their services and often have trouble setting prices.

Inseparability refers to the fact that the service cannot be separated from the person providing it. The quality of service is unique and dependent on the skills of the service provider. This is because the client must participate in the production of the service.

Services are **perishable** because they cannot be inventoried, returned, or resold. Sales lost during off-peak times represent revenue that is lost forever.

Services are **variable** because they are not performed in the same way each and every time. This raises the level of perceived risk for buyers of services.

5 DISTRIBUTION SYSTEMS

CHANNELS OF DISTRIBUTION

Channels of distribution are designed in response to the needs of the sellers in executing the marketing mix. Environmental factors considered within this context include company resources, buyer behavior, competitors' strategies, and the product itself. Channel structure, the relative intensity of distribution, and the number of members within the channel are among the critical decisions made in establishing a distribution channel.

CHANNEL FUNCTIONS

The physical distribution of products is the primary function served by channels. Distribution includes transportation, inventory management, and customer service functions. Intermediaries can also perform other tasks that contribute to greater channel efficiency and market development. These include market research, promotion, and product planning.

In many channel systems, members participate in the **sorting** process. This includes accumulation, sorting, and assorting functions. **Accumulation** is the process of assembling and pooling relatively small individual shipments so that they can be transported more economically. **Sorting** is the process of separating goods by quality, color, or size. **Assorting** is typically performed at the retail level. It is the process of acquiring a wide variety of merchandise to meet the diverse preferences of consumers.

CHANNEL STRUCTURE

Channel systems that move goods from the producer to the final consumer without using independent intermediaries or "middlemen" are termed **Direct Channels**. Those that move goods with the cooperation and assistance of independent intermediaries are **Indirect Channels**.

Channel width refers to the number of independent members at one level of the distribution channel (e.g., producer, wholesaler, retailer, final consumer). **Channel length** refers to the number of levels used to create a distribution channel.

The intensity of a distribution system is determined by the number of intermediaries involved at the wholesale and retail levels of the channel. An **Intensive** distribution strategy is one in which a firm sells through every potential outlet that will reach its target market. With **Selective** distribution, a firm will sell through many, but not all, potential wholesalers and retailers. An **Exclusive** distribution strategy limits the number of outlets employed to one or two intermediaries within each market.

Three types of systems can be used to coordinate distribution functions within indirect channels. In a **Corporate** channel of distribution, one firm owns either all channel members or the firms at the next level in the channel. The control of operations within the channel is maintained through ownership.

Two arrangements can be used to coordinate the functions of independent members within indirect channels. **Contractual** arrangements specify performance terms for each independent channel member. Legal contracts specify terms governing the matters related to the physical movement of goods, pricing policies, and system efficiency. **Administered** arrangements coordinate channel operations through a dominant channel member. The market power of the dominant firm is sufficient to secure the voluntary cooperation of other channel members.

Vertical Integration is the process of acquiring firms that operate at different channel levels. One possible outcome of this strategy is the development of a corporate channel system. In this instance, vertical integration has the effect of increasing operational control and stability of the channel. **Horizontal Integration** is the process of acquiring firms that operate at the same channel level. This strategy allows the firm to increase its competitive strength, market share, and power within the channel system.

MULTIPLE CHANNELS

Multiple Channels (also called dual distribution) exist when a firm develops two or more separate and distinct distribution channels. This strategy may be pursued for several reasons. The firm may use multiple channels as a means of increasing market coverage or to reach new market segments. New channels may also be created to distribute new products.

CHANNEL BEHAVIOR

Channel Control refers to the ability to influence the actions of other channel members. This control may be established by the decision-making structure of the channel (e.g., corporate ownership) or from the relative market power of the members.

Channel Conflict exists when disagreements arise between members over channel practices and policies. Horizontal conflicts take place between firms at the same channel level. Vertical conflict occurs between firms at different levels of the same distribution system.

PUSHING vs. PULLING STRATEGIES

Manufacturers have two strategy alternatives to consider as a means of ensuring that products (especially new products) reach the final consumer. **Pushing** a product through the channel utilizes promotional efforts to secure the cooperation of intermediaries. Sales promotions, personal selling, and advertising are directed toward persuading intermediaries to cooperate in the marketing of the product. A **Pulling** strategy generates consumer demand for the product as a means of securing support within the channel. Promotional efforts are initially directed toward the final consumer. Pulling is most appropriate for new products seeking to gain access to an existing channel.

PHYSICAL DISTRIBUTION SYSTEMS

The most fundamental physical distribution tasks are transportation, materials handling, order processing, and inventory management. The goals of physical distribution systems are most critically concerned with two interrelated issues: costs and customer service. Cost control and reduction can be achieved through more efficient transportation practices and improved inventory management. Customer service and customer satisfaction depends on the efficient processing of orders and the reliable delivery of goods.

The **Total-Cost Concept** recognizes that minimizing costs and satisfying customer demands can represent conflicting objectives. The goal of the Total-Cost approach to system efficiency is to provide a level of customer service at the lowest total costs. These costs include lost sales resulting from customer dissatisfaction. The Total-Cost Concept takes into account that sacrificing some marginal sales opportunities can result in lower total system costs. Consequently, the ideal physical distribution system must strike a balance that preserves both high sales opportunities, customer satisfaction, and the lowest possible distribution costs.

Providing one centrally located stock of inventory for all markets provides for better inventory control, requires less total inventory, and reduces handling costs. This strategy may, however, create very high transportation costs and delivery delays for customers. Using too many dispersed inventory sites poses the opposite problems.

The **Distribution-Center Concept** recognizes that the most effective strategy may be a compromise between these two extremes. The resulting **distribution centers** are a type of warehouse planned in relation to specific markets. They provide key locations at which all operations take place. Each center is an integrated system that takes orders, processes them, and makes delivery to the customer.

Suboptimization refers to cost-reducing actions in one distribution function that increase the overall cost of other distribution functions.

Customer Service Standard refers to different customers requiring different levels of service. Service needs vary from buyer to buyer and sellers need to analyze and adapt to customer preferences. The basic dimensions that relate to customer service in distribution include fair prices, dependable product delivery, timeliness, availability, adequacy of inventory in stock, efficient order processing, replacement of defective goods, and warranties.

Order Processing refers to the receipt and transmission of sales order information. The primary tasks involved in order processing include order entry, order handling, and order delivery. **Electronic Data Interchange** (EDI) allows a company to integrate order processing, production, inventory planning, and transportation into a single system.

Materials Handling refers to the physical handling of goods in both warehouse and transportation functions. **Unit loading** refers to the grouping of boxes on a pallet or skid. **Containerization** is the process of consolidating many items into one container.

Warehousing is the process of designing and operating facilities for both storing and moving goods. Warehouse functions include receiving, sorting, storing, and dispatching goods. **Types of warehouses** include private and public warehouses, distribution centers, and bonded storage. Concepts related to the efficient operation of warehouses and warehouse inventory management include:

> **Order Leadtime** – the average length of time between the customer placing an order and receiving it
>
> **Reorder Point** – the inventory level at which new orders need to be placed to avoid a stockout
>
> **Stockout** – a shortage of product resulting from carrying too few in inventory

Usage Rate – the rate at which inventory is sold per time period

Safety Stock – the amount of extra inventory kept on hand to avoid stockouts

Economic Order Quantity (EOQ) – the order size that minimizes the total cost of ordering and carrying inventory

Just-in-Time (JIT) – making products and materials available just as needed for production or resale

Transportation Modes – the means of moving goods from one location to another. The five major modes are railroads, trucks, waterways, airways, and pipelines.

Megacarriers – freight transport companies that provide several shipment modes

Intermodal Transportation – two or more transportation modes used in combination

Freight Forwarders – specialized agencies that provide alternate forms of transportation coordination

6 WHOLESALING AND RETAILING

WHOLESALING

Wholesaling consists of all the activities related to the resale of products to organizational buyers, other wholesalers, and retailers. These functions typically include warehousing, transporting, and financing. Wholesalers participate in the sorting process by accumulating an assortment of merchandise and redistributing large product volumes in smaller units. Wholesalers provide a sales force that enables manufacturers to reach many customers at relatively low costs.

Manufacturer Wholesaling exists when the product's producer performs the wholesaling functions. These are carried out through the manufacturer's branch offices and sales offices. **Merchant Wholesalers** are independent firms that take title and possession of the products they sell. These firms are sometimes referred to as distributors or jobbers. Merchant wholesalers may be full- or limited-service wholesalers.

Full Service Merchant Wholesalers perform the complete range of wholesaling functions. They store, promote, and transport merchandise. They provide sales support, merchandising assistance, customer service, and market research information to both their suppliers and customers. They can often provide assistance in financing transactions by extending trade credit. **Limited Service Merchant Wholesalers** may not provide merchandising or market research assistance. In most instances, they will not extend credit to facilitate transactions.

Rack Jobbers are full-service merchant wholesalers that provide the display racks used to merchandise the product. **Drop Shippers** are limited-service merchant wholesalers that buy products from manufacturers and arrange for the delivery to retailers. They take title of the merchandise, but do not take physical possession of it.

Agents are independent wholesalers that do not take title of the products that they handle. They derive their compensation through sales commissions or manufacturer fees. **Brokers** act as temporary wholesalers. Their primary function is to bring buyers and sellers together and facilitate the transaction process. They do not take title of merchandise.

RETAILING

Retailing consists of all the activities related to the sale of products to final consumers for individual or household consumption. Retailers are the final link in the channel of distribution.

There are three forms of **Ownership** that can be used to classify retailers. **Corporate Chains** are comprised of several (usually 10 or more) stores that are owned and managed by the same firm. They are typically standardized with respect to product lines, merchandising, and operational policies.

Vertical Marketing Systems provide a collective means of enhancing the market power of individually owned retail units. Vertical Marketing Systems (VMS's) link stores together in voluntary chains or cooperatives. These contractual arrangements allow the group to compete more effectively and provide members with the advantages enjoyed by chain stores. The VMS provides members with assistance in merchandising, personnel training, inventory management, accounting, and promotion.

Independent Stores are single retail units that are not affiliated with a corporate chain or cooperative. They tend to have higher prices than affiliated stores, less market power, and rely more heavily on customer service for a competitive edge.

Franchise Systems are a specific type of Vertical Marketing System. Under this form of VMS, the parent company (franchisor) provides franchisees with the legal right to use company trademarks. The franchisor may also provide franchisees with assistance in site selection, personnel training, inventory management, and promotional strategy. This system allows franchisees to take advantage of well-known product and brand names. Participants may also benefit from the direct acquisition of proven store layouts and operational procedures.

Retail stores may pursue one of several store mix strategies. These strategies are based on product assortment, pricing strategy, and the level of customer service provided. The table below classifies each store according to the width and depth of its product assortment, pricing strategy, and level of customer service relative to other store types selling similar products.

STORE TYPE	PRODUCT ASSORTMENT	PRICING STRATEGY	CUSTOMER SERVICE
Convenience Store	Narrow/Shallow	High Prices	Low
Supermarket	Wide/Deep	Low/Moderate	Moderate
Department Store	Wide/Deep	Moderate	Moderate/High
Discount Store	Wide/Shallow	Low	Low
Specialty Store	Narrow/Very Deep	High	High
Catalog Showroom	Wide/Shallow	Low	Low
Superstores & Hypermarkets	Very Wide/Deep	Low	Low

Nonstore Retailing describes retail transactions that occur outside of traditional store settings. The techniques of nonstore retailing include direct selling, direct marketing, and vending sales. These activities account for about 20 percent of retail sales.

The selection of a **retail store location** is a function of the target market, location of competitors, and site costs. Location options include planned shopping centers, unplanned business/shopping districts, and isolated store locations.

A store's **atmosphere** is comprised of those characteristics that contribute to consumers' general impression of the store—its image. The dimensions that contribute to store atmosphere include the exterior appearance, interior design, product display, and store layout.

Scrambled Merchandising takes place as retailers add products that are not related to their traditional lines. Retailers engaged in this practice are seeking to add any products that sell quickly, increase profitability, and build store traffic. Scrambled merchandising can attract different target markets and often creates competition between unrelated retail stores.

Wheel of Retailing is a concept that describes the evolution of retail stores. The theory states that new retailers enter markets as low-status, low-price competitors. If successful, they tend to evolve into more traditional forms—adding customer-service features and raising prices to meet higher operating costs. This moving-up process creates opportunities for new retailers to enter the market with "low-end" strategies.

Non-store Retailing or **Direct Marketing** is two-way interaction between a marketer and individual consumers to both obtain an immediate response and cultivate lasting customer relationships. These channels include Internet marketing, catalog marketing, direct mail, infomercials, TV home shopping channels, and other forms of direct marketing. The growth in direct marketing sales over the past decade can be attributed to:

- Consumers' lack of time, combined with the convenience of ordering from direct marketers

- The higher costs of driving, traffic, and parking congestion

- Growth of customer databases in both number and sophistication

- Demassification—the focus on smaller market segments and niches

7 PROMOTIONAL STRATEGY

PROMOTION PLANNING

The process of Promotion Planning requires that the firm identify the most appropriate Promotion Mix, Objectives, and Budget. The Promotion Plan serves to coordinate elements of the firm's promotional efforts with the total marketing program. Elements within the promotional mix must be both internally consistent and jointly supportive of the strategic direction of the other marketing mix variables.

Promotion Mix is comprised of those elements that contribute to the firm's overall communications program. The mix includes advertising, personal selling, publicity, public relations, and sales promotions.

Integrated Marketing Communications (IMC) refers to the concept of planning a comprehensive program that coordinates all promotional activities. IMC programs specify four Ws:

- Who is the target market?

- What are the objectives?

- When should the promotions be run?

- Which media should be used?

Promotion Objectives may address three goals within the marketing mix. Promotion can be used to **inform** both intermediaries and end-users about new products. For products that are already established, promotion can be used to persuade buyers. The objective is to influence brand preference and purchase behavior. Promotion may also serve to **remind** buyers about the availability of very well-established products.

Communication Channels provide the medium through which promotional messages are sent and delivered. The elements of a typical channel of communication are shown on the following page.

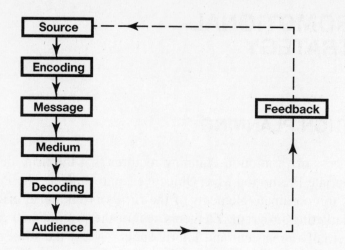

This process may be interfered with or could break down at any point along the sequence due to **noise**. Noise may result in poorly encoded/decoded messages or weak audience response.

Several different techniques can be used to establish promotion **budgets**. The **Percent-of-Sales** technique allocates a fixed percentage of the previous year's sales for promotional programs. The **Competitive Parity** approach establishes a budget based on the actions of the firm's closest competitors. This strategy seeks to mirror rivals' changes in promotional intensity. The **Objective and Task** procedure relies on the matching of promotional objectives to the funding required to achieve specific, objective-related tasks.

New firms often spend as much as they can afford when initially establishing a promotion budget. Once all other elements of the marketing plan have been funded, the **All Available Funds** technique allocates remaining resources to promotional activities.

ADVERTISING PLAN

Advertising **objectives** are determined by the marketing strategy for the product or firm. These objectives may include:

- New Product Introduction—Build Brand Awareness

- Establish Brand Preference (Selective Demand)

- Create and Maintain Brand Loyalty

- Market Development

- Build Primary Demand, Industry Sales

- Increase Product Uses or Rates of Usage

- Support the Firm's Sales Force

- Enhance the Firm's Image

Several of these objectives are typically combined in the development of an advertising plan.

The **Advertising Budget** stems from the budget developed in the Promotion Plan. The determination of a specific dollar allocation reflects the costs associated with alternative media and production costs.

Two different levels of decision making relate to **media planning**: the choice of media-type and the selection of specific vehicles within each medium. Once appropriate vehicles have been identified, the process of developing advertising schedules and buying media begins.

The alternative media available to advertisers include television, radio, newspapers, magazines, outdoor advertising, and direct mail. Each medium has distinctive characteristics that may pose an advantage or problem—depending on the creative requirements of the ad and the nature of the product.

MEDIUM	STRENGTHS	WEAKNESSES
Television	Combines action and sound. Extensive market coverage.	Very expensive. Viewers' short attn. span.
Radio	Station formats can provide access to target markets.	Audio only. Very passive medium.
Newspapers	Flexible—short lead times. Concentrated market.	Poor-quality printing. High ad clutter.
Magazines	High-quality color printing. Very selective means of access to specific audiences. Long life, good pass-along value.	Less flexible scheduling of ads—long lead times.
Outdoor Ads	High-intensity coverage within geographic market area. Large size, brief messages.	Low impact. Public criticism of "landscape pollution."
Direct Mail	Highly selective—no wasted circulation.	Low rate of consumer acceptance. Very expensive.

The selection of specific vehicles within each medium can be influenced by several factors. The evaluation of alternative vehicles is based on the cost and market coverage measures listed below.

Reach refers to the percentage of a target audience that is exposed to an ad through a given vehicle, within a specified time frame. The time frame used is typically four weeks.

Advertising costs are evaluated according to the cost of reaching a thousand prospects through a given vehicle—**Cost-per-Thousand**. Establishing this common measure of efficiency allows for comparisons across media and within media types.

Frequency refers to the average number of times that members of the target audience are exposed to an ad through a given vehicle. Like Reach, Frequency is usually based on a four-week period.

Gross Rating Points (GRPs) are calculated by multiplying Reach times Frequency. GRPs indicate the "total weight" of advertising delivered over a four-week period.

The **Creative Platform** provides the overall concept and theme for an advertising campaign. Themes may relate to the product, the consumer, or the firm. Product themes emphasize performance characteristics and the brand's competitive advantages. Consumer themes stress benefits of using the brand or illustrate how the product can enhance the buyer's life. Ads emphasizing the firm are typically intended to improve the image of the company.

Advertising Effectiveness can be assessed by both direct and indirect measures. Sales, store traffic, and coupon redemption rates provide direct measures of advertising effects. Indirect measures use consumers' recall of ads to estimate their impact.

PUBLICITY AND PUBLIC RELATIONS

Publicity is a form of nonpersonal communication that is not paid for by an identified sponsor. Publicity efforts initiated by firms include news features, articles in business and trade publications, and editorials. Publicity about a firm may be either positive or negative. The content of publicity pieces can be influenced, but not controlled, by a firm. Both positive and negative publicity is characterized by high audience attentiveness and high credibility.

Public Relations may be paid or nonpaid and includes both personal and nonpersonal communications. Public relations is primarily concerned with enhancing the image of the firm. Institutional advertising, personal appearances, and publicity represent various forms of public relations.

PERSONAL SELLING

There are three types of salespeople corresponding to the essential tasks of personal selling. **Order Getters** are responsible for securing new business for the firm. **Order Takers** service customer accounts that have already been established.

There are two types of **Support Salespeople** who provide assistance to both the order getters and order takers. Missionary salespeople work for producers. They foster goodwill and work to maintain productive relationships with intermediaries and their customers. Technical Specialists support the efforts of order getters and order takers by providing customers with expert technical assistance.

The process of recruiting salespeople begins with determining the number of people needed and the qualifications desired. These factors may include education, intelligence, technical knowledge/skills, job experience, and personality traits. Based on a written job description, a pool of qualified applicants is reviewed and the best qualified candidates should be selected.

Sales force training programs differ, according to the needs of the employer. Virtually all salespeople need some training. The most fundamental issues in training programs include company policies, product information, and selling techniques.

Sales potential, the maximum possible sales within a territory, will vary according to several considerations. Some of these factors include the number of potential buyers, the size of accounts, the relative dispersion of buyers, and the geographic characteristics of the market.

Sales Force Allocation to specific territories should attempt to match the talent and ability of salespeople to the characteristics of the customers within the territory. Ideally, each salesperson should be assigned to the territory where his or her relative contribution to the firm's profitability is the greatest. Sales managers will endeavor to minimize the ratio of selling expense to total sales for each territory.

Selling Process is a sequence of stages that are essential to effective personal selling.

Prospecting is the process of seeking and identifying prospective buyers or "leads." In addition, the prospect must be "qualified" to buy. In **Qualifying Leads** the salesperson determines whether the prospect is both willing and able to buy.

The **Pre-Approach** takes place prior to meeting with a qualified prospect, when the salesperson must decide how to best initiate a face-to-face meeting. This includes an analysis of available information about the prospect's buying behavior and an evaluation of competitors' products.

The **Approach** takes place when the seller first meets the prospective buyer. The goal at this stage is to gain the interest and attention of the buyer. Since there are several possible strategies that can be effective, careful pre-approach planning should indicate which ones are most likely to succeed.

The **Presentation** of the sales message may take the form of a prepared ("canned") presentation or take an interactive (needs-satisfaction) approach. The message is intended to persuade buyers to purchase based on the attributes and benefits of the seller's product.

Meeting Objections, part of the presentation process, is an important sales skill. Objections raised by a prospect may represent a request for clarification or additional information. Well-prepared salespeople will anticipate objections and be prepared to overcome them.

Closing the Sale is the stage at which the seller tries to gain a purchase commitment from the prospect. Salespeople who are uncertain that it is an appropriate time to "close the deal" may use a trial close. If a trial close seems to be going well, it can be pursued to a complete close. If not, it can be withdrawn without detracting from the effectiveness of the meeting.

The **Follow-Up** step in the process represents the salesperson's efforts to assure customer satisfaction after the sale. These efforts provide an important basis for building goodwill and future sales. It may also be used to suggest additional sales of the product or related goods.

Canned sales presentations are memorized messages. Salespeople using canned presentations deliver the same prepared statement to each prospect. **Interactive** presentations rely heavily on learning more about each prospect's needs and preferences through direct interaction. Salespeople using this "needs-satisfaction" approach tailor each sales message to each customer. By allowing the potential buyer to speak initially about his or her needs, the salesperson can respond by explaining how the product will address those needs. It is a problem-solving approach to selling. Many salespeople employ parts of both strategies.

Relationship Selling refers to those salesperson's activities that are focused on building ties to the customer. Paying attention to buyer's needs and being truly committed to the customer's satisfaction are the key components of relationship selling.

Partnership Selling refers to formal arrangements between buyers and sellers that create unique, customized products and services for the buyer. This often requires each party to share their unique knowledge and expertise with the other in ways that are not characteristic of conventional buyer-seller relationships. This includes disclosing sensitive competitive and company information, as well as providing access to each other's technical experts.

Sales Force Structure refers to how sellers choose to organize their sales force. A sales force can be organized according to geographic territories, product lines, or customer types. Companies may have both **inside** and **outside** sales forces. Inside salespeople conduct business from their offices via telecommunications media or meet with clients at the seller's location. Outside salespersons travel to make sales calls on customers.

Salesforce Compensation plans may take one of three basic forms: **Straight Salary**, **Straight Commission**, or **A Combination Plan**. The appropriateness of each option is determined by balancing the need to provide income security (salary) versus sales incentives (commission). Combination Plans provide for some measure of both.

The **Drawing Account Method** is a modification of the straight commission plan. Under this method, sales commissions are credited to each individual's drawing account. Salespeople may withdraw a fixed amount each period against their current balance or as an advance against future commissions. In most instances, employees are responsible for any indebtedness incurred under this plan. Some employers, however, provide a **guaranteed draw** where the salesperson is not obligated to pay back the difference when the draw exceeds commissions earned over a specified period.

A great deal of information about the performance of salespeople can be obtained from Sales Reports. Sales Reports describe each individual's schedule of calls and sales results. Key measures of a salesperson's performance include revenue per call, number of calls per day, time per contact, cost per call, percentage of "successes" per call, and the number of new customers created.

Ratios are often used in the **evaluation process**. Among the most common evaluation ratios are Sales/Sales Potential, Sales Expense/Sales, Total Accounts/Total Potential Number of Accounts, and Total Number of Calls/Number of Accounts. Comparisons may be made to the same salesperson's performance in previous periods or to the performance standards established by others.

Qualitative measures are also used to evaluate salespeople. Customer satisfaction can be measured through telephone interviews or mail questionnaires. Many firms also provide for formal assessment of salespeople's knowledge of the company, its products, customers, and competitors.

SALES PROMOTION

Sales Promotion is comprised of all paid marketing communications other than advertising, public relations, and personal selling. In contrast to advertising, sales promotions are usually intended to provide short-term boosts in product sales. The types of sales promotions typically aimed at final consumers and intermediaries are listed below.

Consumer-Directed—Coupons, Contests, Sweepstakes, Rebates, Premiums, Refunds, Point-of-Purchase Displays, Product Samples, Trading Stamps, Cents-Off Deals, Multi-Pack Offers, Demonstrations, Free Trial Offers

Intermediary-Directed—Push Money, Trade Allowances, Quantity Discounts, Sales Contests, Trade Shows, Point-of-Purchase Display Materials, Trade Rebates

DIRECT MARKETING

Direct Marketing refers to one-on-one communications with targeted customers and is aimed primarily at obtaining an immediate response. Direct marketing media include catalogs, direct mail, telemarketing, infomercials, faxes, email, and online Internet services. Companies engaged in direct marketing collect comprehensive data about customers and prospects in electronic **databases**. These databases typically contain information about prior purchase behavior, demographics, psychographics, and geographic data.

Online Marketing refers to all marketing activities conducted through interactive online computer networks or systems that link buyers and sellers. The Internet is the dominant online marketing channel. **Electronic Commerce** is the term used to describe all forms of buying and selling that is supported by electronic means. The benefits of online marketing to both buyers and sellers are summarized in the table below.

BUYERS	SELLERS
Convenience (no driving, parking, etc.)	Good tools for building relationships
Private	Opportunity to learn more about buyers
Abundance of Choices (multiple sellers)	Customize product offering to buyer needs
Time Savings	Access to a truly global marketplace
Interactive (site provides info and options)	Reduced costs—increased efficiency
Immediate	Flexible—website is easily changed

8 PRICING POLICIES AND STRATEGIES

PRICE ELASTICITY OF DEMAND

Price elasticity of demand is the percentage change in the number of units demanded divided by the percentage change in the price of the product. It reflects the degree to which the level of product sales is dependent on price. Specifically, it relates the rate at which demand changes in response to price changes. The mathematical formula for price elasticity of demand is shown below.

$$\text{Price Elasticity of Demand} = \frac{(Q_1 - Q_2)/Q_1 + Q_2}{(P_1 - P_2)/P_1 + P_2}$$

Where:
Q_1 = Initial Quantity Demanded
Q_2 = New Quantity Demanded
P_1 = Initial Price
P_2 = New Price

Elastic Demand exists when the value of the price elasticity of demand formula is less than –1. If demand is elastic, an increase in price will produce a decrease in demand and a decrease in total revenue. (Total Revenue is the product of price times the number of units sold.) Price decreases will increase demand and **increase** total revenue.

Inelastic Demand exists when the value of the price elasticity of demand formula is greater than –1. If demand is inelastic, an increase in price will produce a decrease in demand and an **increase** in total revenue. Price decreases will increase demand and **decrease** total revenue. If demand does not decrease at all in response to price increases, it is said to be perfectly inelastic.

Unitary Elasticity exists when the value of the price elasticity of demand formula is –1. In this instance, the change in demand is directly proportional to the change in price. When unitary elasticity exists, total revenue does not change in response to price increases or decreases.

The **Price Elasticity of Demand Coefficient (E_d)** is equal to the **absolute value** or non-negative value of the Price Elasticity of Demand formula (shown on the previous page). The interpretation of E_d is provided in the table below.

Value of E_d	Effect of an Increase in Price on Quantity Demanded (Q_d) and Total Revenue (*TR*)
If $E_d = 0$ (Perfectly Inelastic)	No Change in Q_d, *TR* Increases
If $E_d < 1$ (Inelastic)	Q_d Decreases, *TR* Increases
If $E_d = 1$ (Unitary Elasticity)	Q_d Decreases, No Change in *TR*
If $E_d > 1$ (Elastic)	Q_d Decreases, *TR* Decreases
If $E_d = \infty$ (Perfectly Elastic)	$Q_d = 0$, *TR* $= 0$

The price elasticity of demand for a given product may change significantly at different price levels. Consequently, the value of E_d should be evaluated at several different prices.

PRICE FIXING AND PRICE DISCRIMINATION

The Sherman Act (1890) prevents businesses from restraining trade and interstate commerce. Pricing policies that are predatory or otherwise contribute to the monopolization of markets and conspiracies contrary to competitive pricing are illegal under the provisions of this law.

The Robinson-Patman Act (1936) prohibits any form of price discrimination that has the effect of reducing competition among wholesalers or retailers. The law provides that the same seller cannot provide the same products to competing buyers (resellers) at different prices unless those price differentials can be justified on the basis of cost savings or good faith efforts to meet competitors' prices. The Robinson-Patman Act also prohibits producers from providing a higher level of service to large customers.

PRICING STRATEGY

Price Skimming is a strategy that introduces new products at relatively high prices. Higher initial prices enhance the perceived quality of the product and maintain demand at a level consistent with the firm's production capacity. The higher profit margins may offset some R&D costs and protect the firm from failing to cover costs.

After the initial introductory period, the firm often lowers its price gradually in response to competitive pressures and the need to reach new market segments. In this way the firm can "skim" layers of profitability from each successive price level. Initially, high prices are paid by the least price-sensitive segment of the market. Lowering product prices over time provides the expansion of the market and growth.

Penetration Pricing is an alternative pricing strategy for new product introductions. This option uses low introductory prices to gain a large share of the market more quickly than price skimming would allow. This is especially appropriate for new products that are very similar to competing brands. The lower price strategy may have several advantages. It provides for quick entry into new markets and often discourages potential competitors from entering. Building relatively high volume sales can also reduce the firm's unit costs through economies of scale. The disadvantages stem from lower unit profit margins and less pricing flexibility.

PRICING DECISIONS

Pricing decisions are often characterized as belonging to one of three categories: cost-based, demand-based, or competition-based pricing. In practice, most pricing decisions integrate elements from each of these categories. Prices typically reflect marketers' consideration of product-related costs, consumer preferences, and competitors' prices.

Cost-Based Pricing establishes product prices as a function of product costs. Cost-based pricing techniques include cost-plus pricing and return-on-investment pricing. Cost-plus pricing determines prices by adding a predetermined level of profit to product costs. Return-on-investment pricing sets product prices that will enable the firm to achieve a specified rate of return. This method requires forecasting sales volume over the life of the investment period. Virtually all price-setting strategies must take costs into account as part of the process.

Demand-Based Pricing attempts to set prices based on consumer responses to product prices. Demand-based pricing techniques include prestige pricing, odd-even pricing, price lining, and leader pricing. These methods of setting prices are sometimes referred to as psychological pricing. Market research on consumer attitudes and preferences often identify the range of acceptable prices specific to each market segment.

Competition-Based Pricing sets prices according to those charged by the firm's closest competitors. This may result in prices above, below, or at market levels. Competition-based pricing strategies include customary pricing and price leadership. In certain markets, competitors have converged on a narrow range of price points. This traditional basis for setting prices is referred to as Customary Pricing. Price Leadership exists when one firm is usually the first to change prices from previous levels and this change is routinely followed by the rest of the industry.

A **One-Price** policy offers the same price to all buyers for purchases of essentially the same quantities in comparable situations. **Flexible Pricing** permits the seller to charge different prices to different buyers in similar circumstances. This strategy is most common in personal selling contexts. Flexible pricing allows the salesperson to adjust prices in response to competitive shifts and customer requirements.

Geographic Pricing policies reflect different levels of transportation and other costs related to the physical distance between buyers and sellers. Sellers may quote F.O.B. (free-on-board) prices, which do not include shipping charges. Zone pricing sets separate prices for different geographic regions—incorporating average transport costs for each area into the quoted prices of the product.

Unit Pricing provides consumers with information on the price per unit on or near the product. This practice is intended to simplify comparisons between brands and various package sizes.

With **alternative pricing objectives,** a firm's pricing strategy may reflect short-term goals other than profit maximization. Short-term price reductions may be intended to build market share, build brand awareness in a new market or segment, change customers' perceptions of product value, move inventory, gain distributor acceptance, or accelerate the pace of new product adoption.

PRICE-QUALITY CORRELATION

In many instances, consumers believe that higher prices represent superior product quality. In the absence of specific product information, buyers often rely on price as an indicator of quality and use this measure when evaluating brands. This price-quality correlation is strongest when buyers have little confidence in their ability to judge product quality and they suspect substantial differences in quality between brands.

PSYCHOLOGICAL PRICING

Prestige Pricing establishes retail prices that are high, relative to competing brands. The higher price is intended to suggest higher product quality, consistent with the strength of the price-quality association in consumers' minds. It may also provide the product with a measure of prestige or status relative to competing brands.

Odd-Even Pricing sets prices just below even dollar values (e.g., $99.99 or $99 v. $100). There are several possible explanations for consumers' apparent preference for certain odd prices, rather than even ones. Buyers may implicitly believe that odd prices are the consequence of a price reduction from a higher even price. They may prefer odd prices because they seem substantially lower (the difference between $100 and $99 seems far more than one dollar). It may also provide shoppers with a reference point when trying to stay within price limits. On balance, consumers seem to feel that odd prices provide greater value for their money.

Consumers may also seek "even" prices under some circumstances. When prices for a product category (e.g., candy bars, chewing gum) have remained relatively stable over extended periods, buyers may have very adverse reactions to any increase. When confronted with rising costs, marketers may try to maintain these **customary prices** by reducing the size of each package or changing the ingredients used in production.

Price Lining simplifies consumers' evaluation of alternative products by establishing a limited number of price points for groups or lines of products. Product groups of similar quality are all sold at the same price, thereby allowing shoppers to evaluate alternatives based on other considerations. A retailer may, for example, price various styles and lines of shirts at three price levels: $24, $29, and $36.

When establishing a price line, the seller must be certain that price points are far enough apart so that buyers perceive different levels of merchandise quality. Price lining may minimize consumers' confusion when comparing brands while allowing retailers to maintain a wider assortment within specified price ranges.

Leader Pricing occurs when a firm sells select products below their usual price as a means of gaining attention or building store traffic. In retail settings, leader pricing tends to feature popular brands of frequently purchased products. The expectation is that sales of regularly priced merchandise will benefit from increased traffic and that the image of the store as a price leader will be enhanced. When items are sold below cost, they are termed "loss leaders."

PROFIT MARGIN

Markups are percentages or dollar amounts added to the cost of sales to arrive at the product's selling price. Many retailers and wholesalers use a standard percentage markup to set selling prices. Markups are usually calculated as a percentage of the selling price, rather than a percentage of the cost.

$$\text{Markup Percentage (On Selling Price)} = \frac{\text{Selling Price} - \text{Product Cost}}{\text{Selling Price}}$$

Example: Product Cost = $50   Selling Price = $80

$$\text{Markup Percentage (On Selling Price)} = \frac{\$80 - \$50}{\$80} = \frac{\$30}{\$80} = .375 \text{ or } 37.5\%$$

$$\text{Selling Price} = \frac{\text{Product Cost}}{(100 - \text{Markup Percent})/100}$$

Example: Product Cost = $30   Markup Percentage = 60%

$$\text{Selling Price} = \frac{\$30}{(100 - 60)/100} = \frac{\$30}{.4} = \$75$$

Markdowns are retail price reductions. Managers typically markdown retail prices in response to low consumer demand. Like markups, markdowns are usually expressed as a percentage of the selling price.

$$\text{Markdown Percentage (Off Original Price)} = \frac{\text{Original Selling Price} - \text{Reduced Price}}{\text{Original Selling Price}}$$

Example: Original Selling Price = $85   Reduced Price = $60

$$\text{Markdown Percentage (Off Original Price)} = \frac{\$85 - \$60}{\$85} = .294 \text{ or } 29.4\%$$

Discounts are reductions from list prices that are given by sellers to buyers. These price reductions may be based on several factors.

Trade Discounts are reductions from the list price given to intermediaries in exchange for the performance of specified tasks. Trade discounts may compensate buyers for promotional considerations, transportation, storage costs, extending credit, and order processing.

Quantity Discounts arise from the economies and improved efficiency of selling in large quantities. As order size increases, the fixed costs related to order processing and customer service remain substantially unchanged. Consequently, the associated per unit costs are reduced for the seller. In turn, some financing and storage costs may also be shifted to the buyer. Quantity discounts may be cumulative over a specified period of time or noncumulative.

Cash Discounts are given to encourage buyers to provide payment promptly. For example, 2/10 net 30 is a common policy that gives buyers a two percent discount if the account is paid within 10 days. "Net 30" indicates that the balance is due within 30 days. If the account is not paid within 30 days, interest may be charged.

Seasonal Discounts are used to encourage buyers to make their purchases off-season. This strategy may provide needed cash to the seller, reduce inventories, or help to smooth out production scheduling.

Allowances are price reductions that are intended to achieve specific goals. Trade-in allowances may make financing a purchase easier for the buyer. Promotional allowances are used to secure reseller participation in advertising and sales support programs intended to boost product sales.

Break-Even Analysis allows managers to estimate the impact of alternative price levels on profits. The Break-Even Point is the price at which total revenue just equals total costs. When sales exceed the break-even level for a given price, each successive unit sold generates profit.

Total Revenue = Price x Quantity Sold

Total Costs = Fixed Costs + (Variables Cost per Unit x Quantity Sold)

$$\text{Break-Even Point (Units)} = \frac{\text{Total Fixed Costs}}{\text{Price} - \text{Variable Cost Per Unit}}$$

Each price level has its own break-even point. The value of break-even analysis stems from its usefulness in evaluating pricing options. It should not, however, be relied on as the sole basis for setting prices. The assumptions implicit in using straight line total revenue and total cost curves are not realistic. If they were, profits would continue to grow indefinitely once the break-even point was surpassed. Break-even analysis represents one additional perspective on price setting that should be incorporated with other cost-based, demand-based, and competition-based pricing strategies.

9 SPECIAL TOPICS IN MARKETING

INTERNATIONAL MARKETING

Any firm that markets products outside its own country is engaged in international marketing. The essentials of marketing are applicable throughout the world. Success in international marketing is contingent on creating a marketing mix that matches the needs and preferences of the target market. The complexity of international marketing operations stems from the need to understand differences between countries and cultures. Among the cultural differences that may impact the marketing plan of a firm are language, family structure, social customs, religion, and educational systems. Government policies may also pose substantial barriers to trade with other countries.

There are several types of intermediaries that can be used to enter foreign markets. Firms may engage the services of import-export intermediaries who provide expertise in international operations. This option requires very little investment on the part of the exporter. Firms willing to commit more resources to international ventures may establish company-owned sales branches in foreign countries. Firms committed to operations in a foreign country may establish wholly-owned foreign subsidiaries.

NONPROFIT MARKETING

Marketing principles and practices are applied within a wide range of nonprofit organizations. Nonprofit marketing applications include the marketing of **Persons**, **Ideas**, and **Organizations**. In contrast to business firms, nonprofit organizations pursue nonfinancial, social, and service objectives. They also differ from "for-profit" ventures by their need to attract volunteer labor and financial contributions. Consequently, nonprofit groups need to satisfy two distinct target markets: donors/supporters and clients/recipients of their services. In addition, their objectives often include gaining the approval and support of society at-large for their causes as well as their organizations.

HISTORY OF THE MARKETING CONCEPT

The Production Era. Beginning in the second half of the nineteenth century, electricity, rail transportation, division of labor, assembly lines, and other mass production concepts made it possible to manufacture goods more efficiently. The prevailing business philosophy of the era emphasized economies of scale in production, improved efficiency, cost containment, and the principles of scientific management.

The Sales Era. From the mid-1920s through the 1950s, the emphasis of the prevailing business philosophy was on sales as the primary means of increasing profits. Personal selling and advertising were regarded as the most important marketing functions.

The Marketing Era. By the early 1950s, many businesses recognized that efficient production and extensive promotion did not guarantee that customers would buy what was being sold. Businesses turned their attention to understanding and serving customers' needs. This emphasis on customer satisfaction resulted in increased concerns about ethics and social responsibility.

THE ROLE OF MARKETING IN THE ECONOMY

Individuals and organizations engage in marketing activities to facilitate exchanges. For an exchange to take place, these four conditions must exist:

1. Two or more individuals or organizations must participate

2. Each party must possess something of value that the other wants to acquire

3. Each party must be willing to give up something of value to acquire something of value

4. Both parties must be able to communicate with each other

Exchanges should satisfy both buyer and seller.

Marketing activities help promote exchanges and produce the profits that are essential to the survival of individual companies and the overall health of the economy. Approximately one-half of buyers' expenditures on products go to cover marketing-related costs.

MARKETING ETHICS

Marketing Ethics are the moral principles that define right and wrong behavior in marketing practice. Many organizations formalize rules and standards of ethical conduct that define what is expected of its employees. These **codes of conduct** are intended to eliminate opportunities for unethical behavior that will reflect badly on the organization.

Ethical models of marketing behavior can be either **compensatory** or **noncompensatory** in nature. Compensatory models are those where the moral right or wrong of an action is determined by the consequences the action produces. "Right action is that which maximizes the good." Noncompensatory models are those that maintain a universally true moral principle with no exceptions. These rules do not allow for considering the consequences of an act. These ethical rules have three tenets: no exceptions to the rule; the principle is impartial; and, it must be consistently applied.

Social Responsibility refers to the firm's obligations to society. Social responsibility has four dimensions: economic, legal, ethical, and philanthropic. The ideal for a socially responsible organization is to maximize the positive impacts and minimize the negative impacts of the firm, while it is operating within its own best interests.

Green Marketing refers to the design, development, and marketing of products that do not harm the environment. Green Marketing initiatives emphasize efforts to reduce or eliminate waste in the production and distribution of products. **Reverse logistics** is a concept that emphasizes the responsibility of the firm for products after they are disposed of by consumers. Recycling and salvaging usable materials from discarded products is a key concept in reverse logistics.

PRACTICE
TEST 1

CLEP PRINCIPLES OF MARKETING
Test 1

(Answer sheets appear in the back of this book.)

TIME: 90 Minutes
100 Questions

DIRECTIONS: Each of the questions or incomplete statements below is followed by five possible answers or completions. Select the best choice in each case and fill in the corresponding oval on the answer sheet.

---

1. The production of a new car model includes which of the following activities?

    (A) Predicting the types of cars different types of people will buy

    (B) Actually making the car

    (C) Determining the features of the car

    (D) Selling the car

    (E) Developing a sales promotion campaign for the car

2. The term "micro-macro dilemma" means that

    (A) people have a hard time making choices between products

    (B) every economy needs a macro-marketing system but not necessarily a micro-marketing system

    (C) what is good for some producers may not be good for society as a whole

    (D) satisfying a customer's wants and needs is difficult because the consumer may not know what his/her wants and needs are

    (E) it is difficult to determine consumer tastes in the globally diverse marketplace

3. An organized way of continually gathering and analyzing data to provide marketing managers with the most up-to-date information they need to make decisions is called

(A) decision support systems (DSS)

(B) time series models

(C) marketing research

(D) marketing information systems (MIS)

(E) consumer panels

4. Ogden Parts Inc. has named a new sales manager with responsibilities for market planning. Ogden's president thinks the sales manager should sell more parts and outsell the competition. It seems that this company is run as if it were in the

(A) sales era

(B) production era

(C) marketing company era

(D) simple trade era

(E) marketing department era

5. The "four Ps" of a marketing mix are

(A) Product, Price, Profit, Promotion

(B) People, Product, Place, Promotion

(C) Promotion, Production, Price, Place

(D) Product, Price, Place, Promotion

(E) Profit, Place, Price, Product

6. The role of price in a market-directed economy is to

(A) determine the sale prices of clearance items in a retail store

(B) serve as a rough measure of the value of resources used to produce goods and services

(C) ensure no consumer pays prices that are too high

(D) determine the amount of losses that can be sustained by a company

(E) allocate profits to companies even though they may not be providing the most desirable goods and services

7. Which of the following statements about marketing is FALSE?

   (A) Marketing attempts to affect the products and services you buy.

   (B) Marketing does not apply to nonprofit organizations.

   (C) Advertising and sales promotion are marketing functions.

   (D) Marketing can affect the prices you will pay for a product.

   (E) Marketing includes decisions about how to sell products.

8. Family units in Smallisland Country make all the products they consume. This is an example of

   (A) an economy where marketing is efficient

   (B) a pure market-oriented economy

   (C) a planned economy

   (D) an economy where the role of middlemen is important

   (E) a pure subsistence economy

9. Tariffs are

   (A) taxes on imported products

   (B) predetermined prices planned by several competing companies

   (C) rules on the amount of products that can be imported

   (D) extra money paid to officials for favored status

   (E) illegal in the United States

10. As XYZ Company produces larger quantities of watches, the cost of producing each watch goes down. This is known as

   (A) micro-marketing   (D) marketing concept

   (B) possession utility   (E) transaction efficiency

   (C) economies of scale

11. The Magnuson Act of 1975 says that

   (A) producers of goods must warrant their products as merchantable

   (B) a written warranty reduces the responsibility of a producer

(C)   producers must provide a clearly written warranty

(D)   each product must be identified with a readable electronic code

(E)   goods must be clearly labeled and easy to understand

12.   When marketers focus on comparing their product versus a competitor's product, they

(A)   formulate a SWOT analysis

(B)   should be concerned with total product offering

(C)   look at the relative quality

(D)   Both (B) and (C)

(E)   All of the above

13.   One would consider an intangible deed performed by one party for another party at a cost as a

(A)   supply   (D)   perishable good

(B)   service   (E)   Both (B) and (D)

(C)   good

14.   Which of the following is NOT true about the three types of convenience products (staples, impulse products, and emergency products)?

(A)   Staples are products that are bought routinely, without much thought.

(B)   With impulse products, much of the buyer's behavior affects place utility.

(C)   Customers shop extensively when purchasing these items.

(D)   Emergency products are purchased when urgently needed.

(E)   With staples, branding helps customers cut shopping efforts.

15.   New product planning is becoming increasingly important in a modern economy because

(A)   most profits go to innovators or fast companies that quickly copy products from other companies

(B)   it is not always profitable JUST to sell "me-too" products

(C) the failure rate of new products is becoming increasingly low

(D) every product must pass FTC laws to be bought and sold

(E) All of the above are true

16. A capital item (a necessary element in setting price) is

(A) a building or other type of major equipment

(B) office supplies purchased by the individuals

(C) raw materials that become part of the physical good

(D) long-lasting products that can be depreciated

(E) Both (A) and (D)

17. Which of the following symbols is a trademark?

(A)
MINOLTA

(D) All of the above

(B)

(E) None of the above

(C) BP

18. The practice of tailoring products and marketing programs to suit the needs of specific individuals is called

(A) niche marketing

(D) micro-marketing

(B) mass marketing

(E) macro-marketing

(C) segment marketing

19. Packaging is of importance to marketers because

(A) it provides better shelf placement in grocery stores

(B) packaging costs over 95% of a manufacturer's selling price

(C) the Federal Packaging and Labeling Act holds restrictions on packaging sizes

(D)   new packages can make a difference in a new marketing strategy

(E)   labels are inaccurate, and no one reads them anyway

20.   What level of familiarity exists when a consumer buys paper clips for the office, and she/he does not notice the brand name of the product?

(A)   Brand rejection   (D)   Brand preference

(B)   Brand recognition   (E)   Brand insistence

(C)   Brand nonrecognition

21.   Some customers feel that certain brands of refrigerators are very similar and have the same attributes. By shopping for the best price, or lowest price, what kinds of products are these?

(A)   Specialty products   (D)   Regularly sought products

(B)   Heterogeneous products   (E)   Homogeneous products

(C)   Convenience products

22.   When Progresso makes Cajun gumbo soup for Louisiana and nacho cheese soup for Texas, what kind of segmentation is it practicing?

(A)   Geographic   (D)   Psychographic

(B)   Behavioral   (E)   Political

(C)   Demographic

23.   Which of the following statements is NOT true about the product life cycle?

(A)   As industry sales rise, industry profits also rise.

(B)   Each stage may have a different target market.

(C)   In general, competition tends to move toward pure competition.

(D)   Industry profits start to decrease in market growth.

(E)   Both (A) and (D).

24.   Which statement is correct about the market growth stage?

(A)   Industry profits tend to increase in the beginning of the stage.

(B)   Industry profits decrease toward the end of the stage.

(C) More companies enter into the industry.

(D) Industry sales increase.

(E) All the above are correct statements.

25. All of the following would be ways to segment a market within the category of "psychographic segmentation" EXCEPT

(A) social class

(D) lifestyle

(B) personality

(E) interests

(C) occupation

26. All of the following are considered to be major variables for segmenting markets EXCEPT

(A) geographic

(D) moods

(B) demographic

(E) psychographic

(C) behavioral

27. Mingilton Meats increased the price of their bologna from $2.00 a pound to $3.00 a pound. After doing this they noticed a decrease in total revenue. This is because

(A) the demand for the meat is elastic

(B) the demand for the meat is inelastic

(C) the demand is unitarily elastic

(D) the meat was too old to purchase

(E) Cannot tell from the information given

28. The Yearous Group saw an increase in total revenue when they decreased the price of their golf bags. The marketing manager can assume that the demand is

(A) unitarily elastic

(D) All of the above

(B) elastic

(E) None of the above

(C) inelastic

29. A potato farmer in Alamosa, Colorado, would be likely to have which type of demand for his potato crop?

(A) Inelastic demand

(B) No demand; everyone buys potatoes from Idaho

(C) Elastic demand

(D) Unitary elasticity of demand

(E) All of the above

30. Bob opened a new restaurant featuring "Crab Legs a la Bob." As he experimented with the price of the offering, he found that no matter if he raised or lowered his price, the total revenue from the "Crab Legs a la Bob" stayed the same. He could conclude that his product had what kind of elasticity?

(A) He can draw no conclusions from the information given.

(B) His demand is elastic.

(C) His demand is inelastic.

(D) He has a situation where there is unitary elasticity.

(E) He should sell shrimp.

31. Given the standard commission used in advertising agencies, what would an agency receive for a magazine ad that cost $20,000?

(A) $1,500   (D) $3,000

(B) $1,750   (E) $5,000

(C) $2,000

32. Given the following choices, which is NOT considered a retailing activity?

(A) The Alpha Kappa Psi Fraternity sells coffee to faculty members in the morning at a local college.

(B) Because your car broke down, you are forced to call a tow truck to tow your car to be fixed, for which you are charged $50.

(C) A soap company salesperson comes to your door and sells you $10 worth of soap.

(D) You purchase a new suit at Macy's Department Store for $259.

(E) All of the above are examples of retailing.

33. If a firm were to obtain information about light, medium, and heavy users of a product as a means to segment their market, the firm would be practicing what kind of segmentation?

    (A) Geographic   (D) Psychographic

    (B) Behavioral   (E) Geodemographic

    (C) Demographic

34. Positioning is

    (A) giving a product meaning that distinguishes it from its competition

    (B) occupying a specific place in consumers minds relative to competing products

    (C) not as important as segmentation

    (D) primarily meant for large multinational companies

    (E) Both (A) and (B) are true

35. Disposable diapers, which are not biodegradable, are what type of new product opportunity?

    (A) Desirable products   (D) Deficient products

    (B) Pleasing products   (E) Salutary products

    (C) Performance products

36. Which of the following statements could occur in market maturity?

    (A) Industry sales become stable.

    (B) Profits can increase for an individual company.

    (C) Individual firms drop out of the industry.

    (D) Promotion costs rise.

    (E) All of the above

37. Stetson's use of the American cowboy in its advertising is an example of a positioning strategy based on

    (A) a product attribute   (D) against competition

    (B) the product's users   (E) a product benefit

    (C) a cultural icon

38. John Randall is a purchasing agent for a rather large delivery service. John has just agreed to purchase a 1992 Chevy van from his brother's construction company, although he has never driven it or seen it. This buying approach would be an example of

    (A) description buying

    (B) test buying

    (C) inspection buying

    (D) sampling buying

    (E) negotiated contract buying

39. Which of the following is NOT part of the Multiple Buying Influence, when making a decision to buy a new copy machine in a business?

    (A) General public

    (B) Influencer

    (C) Buyer

    (D) Decider

    (E) Gatekeeper

40. By definition, "Price" is

    (A) the sticker on a product that suggests a price

    (B) what is charged for something (product or service)

    (C) calculated by dividing cost with retail selling price

    (D) the term used by marketers defining the cost of a product

    (E) profit-oriented

41. Sally Rudolph is selling a new shirt, which she made, to her friend for $1,000. The shirt cost Sally $400. What is her markup?

    (A) $40

    (B) $100

    (C) $300

    (D) $400

    (E) $600

42. If Bob Peters sells a set of steak knives for $1,000, and he has a markup (or selling price) of $600, what is his markup percent?

    (A) 10%

    (B) 20%

    (C) 50%

(D)   60%

(E)   Cannot be determined from the information given.

43.   What is the retail price if the cost of a product is $400, and the markup percent on the retail selling price is 60%?

(A) $1,000

(B) $2,000

(C) $450

(D) $550

(E) $600

44.   Ron and Dee own a floor tile retail outlet. They want to achieve a 40% markup at retail for all of the merchandise that they sell. If one style of floor tile retails at $3 per tile, what is the maximum that Ron and Dee can pay for the tile?

(A) $2.06

(B) $2.10

(C) $2.14

(D) $2.22

(E)   Cannot be determined from the information given.

45.   Pake Productions wants to markdown a new line of speakers that they have in the stores. After they are marked down, Pake Productions wants to calculate the markdown percentage. If the original price of the speakers was $200, and the new price of the speakers is $160, what is the markdown percent?

(A) $40

(B) $50

(C)   25%

(D)   20%

(E)   Both (C) and (D) are correct.

46.   Ogden & Ogden receive an invoice for $100, which they pay in nine days. The terms on the invoice indicate 2/10 net 30. How much money did Ogden & Ogden send to the seller?

(A) $100

(B) $98

(C) $102

(D) $2.00

(E) $96.45

47. Making goods and services available in the right quantities and locations when the customer wants them is the definition for which one of the following marketing mix variables?

    (A) Promotion

    (B) Place

    (C) Product

    (D) Price

    (E) None of the above

48. Alarid Company purchases goods from a manufacturer who then turns around and sells them to a retailer who sells them to final customers. The Alarid Company is participating in a(n)

    (A) regrouping activity

    (B) accumulating activity

    (C) channel of distribution

    (D) bulk-breaking project

    (E) None of the above

49. In terms of direct marketing expenses, the second biggest category after telemarketing is

    (A) radio direct response

    (B) television infomercials

    (C) direct mail

    (D) magazine direct marketing

    (E) Internet marketing

50. Which of the following is an important advantage of direct marketing?

    (A) Low cost

    (B) Ability to tailor messages to a specific audience

    (C) Fast response time between placing and shipping the order

    (D) Ability to use just-in-time inventory management

    (E) High rate of consumer acceptance

51. ABC Corporation sells only to wholesalers who give their product special attention. ABC Corporation is practicing what type of distribution?

    (A) Selective distribution

    (B) Intensive distribution

    (C) Exclusive distribution

    (D) Ideal market exposure

    (E) None of the above

52. Public relations firms are often evaluated by the number of "hits" they obtain. A "hit" is

    (A) an advertisement that is successful

    (B) a special event tie-in with publicity

    (C) the mention of a company's name in a news story

    (D) a media story that speaks positively about a company

    (E) a media story that speaks negatively about a company

53. Turner Corporation sells its product to several competing channels that will reach the same target market. Turner Corporation is using what type of distribution?

    (A) Exclusive distribution   (D) Both (A) and (B).

    (B) Intensive distribution   (E) None of the above

    (C) Dual distribution

54. Which statement best describes why Dual Distribution is becoming more common with producers and retailers?

    (A) It is best applicable for convenience products and business suppliers.

    (B) Retailers want large quantities with a lower price per unit.

    (C) Present channel members are doing an excellent job.

    (D) Both (A) and (C).

    (E) All of the above

55. The public relations tool that is mostly internally oriented is the

    (A) press release

    (B) company newsletter

    (C) financial statement

    (D) network television spot

    (E) balance of payments statement

56. What are the two basic types of conflicts in channels of distribution?

    (A) Horizontal and vertical

    (B) Discrepancy of quantity and assortment

    (C) Assorting and sorting

    (D) Both (B) and (C)

    (E) None of the above

57. Within the industrial mix, the product variable places a great deal of emphasis on

    (A) price

    (B) services

    (C) environmental influences

    (D) distribution

    (E) sales promotion

58. In regard to industrial marketing, the following example best exemplifies what type of pricing? "The seller determines the price (or a series of prices) for a given product, and the customer pays that specified price."

    (A) Bid pricing

    (B) Negotiated pricing

    (C) Administered pricing

    (D) Retail pricing

    (E) Economic pricing

59. A "perceptual map" is a marketing tool that helps managers with

    (A) positioning decisions

    (B) product design

    (C) packaging decisions

    (D) deciding where in the country to sell a product

    (E) determining shipping costs

60. Advertising can make industrial customers aware of

    (A) new products or brands

    (B) product features

    (C) organizations

    (D) representatives

    (E) All of the above

61. Which of the following statements is NOT true when developing a marketing strategy?

    (A) It allows flexibility in providing for customer service.

    (B) It allows the hiring of high-quality personnel.

    (C) It may help to resolve problems in regard to service.

    (D) It provides for the use of high technology, allowing for lower cost services.

    (E) None of the above.

62. If an organization is conducting marketing activities other than for the goals of profit, market share, or return on investment (ROI), these marketing activities are referred to as

    (A) a waste of time   (D) promotional marketing

    (B) nonbusiness marketing   (E) nonmarketing activities

    (C) strategic marketing

63. Generally speaking, a department store salesperson who stands behind a counter and performs a cashier's role can be classified as a(n)

    (A) order getter   (D) missionary salesperson

    (B) order taker   (E) copywriter

    (C) public relations specialist

64. What is the key to creating value and customer satisfaction?

    (A) Total quality   (D) Celebrity advertising

    (B) Everyday low prices   (E) Sales promotions

    (C) Manufacturing superiority

65. Which of the following choices is NOT a level in the hierarchy of needs?

    (A) Money needs

    (B) Safety needs

    (C) Physiological needs

    (D) Social needs

    (E) All of the above are levels in the hierarchy of needs.

66. Which of the following choices best defines a change in a person's thought process caused by prior experience?

    (A) Cue

    (B) Response

    (C) Learning

    (D) Belief

    (E) Reinforcement

67. In marketing, an analysis of a person's day-to-day patterns of living is referred to as a person's AIOs, which are also known as

    (A) Awareness, Interests, Opinions

    (B) Activities, Interests, Opinions

    (C) Actions, Incentives, Objections

    (D) Actions, Integrity, Observations

    (E) Awareness, Incentives, Observations

68. The American market is changing and therefore businesses must adapt to these changes. Today, most successful companies are moving away from

    (A) target marketing

    (B) market segmentation

    (C) market positioning

    (D) mass marketing

    (E) direct marketing

69. Carefully arranging for a product or service to occupy a clear, distinctive, and desirable place relative to competing products or services in the minds of target consumers is called

    (A) mass marketing

    (B) target marketing

    (C) market segmentation

    (D) green marketing

    (E) positioning

70. Which of the following is the best example of a product a consumer would consider under the extensive problem-solving process?

    (A) Milk

    (B) Washing machine

    (C) Pair of shoes

    (D) Toilet paper

    (E) T-shirt

71. Which of the following is NOT one of the steps in the adoption process?

    (A) Confirmation   (D) Decision

    (B) Trial   (E) Payment

    (C) Awareness

72. Which of the following is NOT a function of channels of distribution?

    (A) Alleviating discrepancies in assortment

    (B) Alleviating discrepancies in quantity

    (C) Providing customer service

    (D) New product development

    (E) Creating utility

73. Which of the following is NOT a regrouping activity used by channel specialists to adjust discrepancies?

    (A) Assorting   (D) Bulk-Breaking

    (B) Accumulating   (E) Sorting

    (C) Transforming

74. Which of the following is one of the reasons that personal selling can be more effective than advertising in a complex selling situation?

    (A) Personal selling is cheaper on a per contact basis.

    (B) Personal selling can reach more customers within a given time period.

    (C) Personal selling can deal with inelastic demand.

    (D) Personal selling can probe customers to learn more about their needs.

    (E) Only (A) and (B) are true.

75. The combining of two or more stages of the channel under one management, in which each channel member is seen as an extension of their own operations, is described as

(A) strategic alliances

(B) horizontal channel integration

(C) reverse channels

(D) oligopoly

(E) vertical channel integration

76. Which type of distribution would best be used for products such as soap, food, and personal care products when consumers desire wide availability of the products?

(A) Intensive distribution

(B) Exclusive distribution

(C) Vertical distribution

(D) Horizontal distribution

(E) Selective distribution

77. Which type of distribution technique used a single outlet in a fairly large geographic area to distribute a product or service such as Jaguar and Rolls-Royce automobiles?

(A) Selective

(B) Universal

(C) Intensive

(D) Exclusive

(E) None of the above.

78. A major reason why some shoppers are reluctant to make Internet purchases is because of

(A) higher prices

(B) inferior quality

(C) concern about security

(D) greater inconvenience

(E) poor selection

79. Forbidding an intermediary to carry products of a competing manufacturer is known as

(A) tying agreement

(B) monopoly

(C) exclusive dealing

(D) strategic channel alliance

(E) vertical marketing system

80. A coupon on a bottle of Pepsi offering a deal on a bag of potato chips is called

(A) cross-ruff coupon

(D) response offer coupon

(B) scanner-delivered coupon

(E) bounce back coupon

(C) instant redemption coupon

81. Which of the following is the most widely used positioning strategy?

(A) Against a competitor

(D) User's lifestyle

(B) Away from a competitor

(E) User's occupation

(C) Product attribute

82. Which of the following factors is at the core of the marketing concept?

(A) Mass marketing

(D) Low prices

(B) Aggressive selling

(E) Customer satisfaction

(C) Brand preference

83. The strategy of choosing one attribute to excel at or to create competitive advantage is called

(A) overpositioning

(D) relationship marketing

(B) unique selling proposition

(E) concentrated marketing

(C) undifferentiated marketing

84. Which of the following pricing policies seems to be the one favored by e-commerce and Internet-based businesses?

(A) Complementary pricing policies

(B) Dynamic pricing policies

(C) Standard pricing policies

(D) Fixed pricing policies

(E) Prestige pricing

85. Which of the following choices is an example of a manufacturer's brand?

(A) Heinz ketchup   (D) Kenmore appliances

(B) Diehard batteries   (E) All of the above

(C) Craftsman tools

86. A strategy that consists of the seller's development of two or more brands in the same product category is called

(A) brand repositioning decision

(B) brand extension decision

(C) multibrand decision

(D) family brand decision

(E) brand quality decision

87. Setting prices as low as possible typically supports which of the following pricing objectives?

(A) Market share leadership

(B) Product quality leadership

(C) Current profit maximization

(D) Survival

(E) Just-in-time policy

88. Rent, heating and air-conditioning, interest, and executive salaries would all be examples of

(A) standard costs   (D) independent costs

(B) variable costs   (E) monopoly costs

(C) fixed costs

89. Which of the following statements is NOT a reason for downward stretching the product line?

(A) The company is attacked at the high end and decides to counterattack by invading the low end.

(B) The company finds that slower growth is taking place at the high end.

(C) The company at the lower end of the market may want to enter the higher end.

(D) The company initially entered the high end to establish a quality image and intended to roll downward.

(E) The company adds a low-end unit to plug a market hole that would otherwise attract a new competitor.

90. The most important factor pushing marketers toward integrated marketing communication is

(A) increasing competition

(B) decreasing costs of advertising

(C) declining use of sales promotions

(D) spiraling costs of personal selling

(E) increased reliance on one medium of advertising

91. Electronic monitoring systems that link consumers' exposure to TV advertising (measured using television meters) with what they actually buy in stores (measured by store checkout scanners) are called

(A) motivational research systems

(B) single-source data systems

(C) peoplemeters

(D) subliminal research systems

(E) focus group data

92. The two major economic factors that reflect a country's attractiveness as an export market are

(A) industrial structure and income distribution

(B) political stability and attitudes

(C) cultural environment and government bureaucracy

(D) joint venturing and direct investment

(E) contract manufacturing and management contracting

93. Which of the following economies creates a new rich class and a small, but growing, middle-class that both demand new types of imported goods?

(A) Subsistence economy

(B) Raw-material-exporting economy

(C) Industrialized economy

(D) Industrializing economy

(E) None of the above.

94. Whenever possible, smart marketers will take a ____ rather than ____ approach to the marketing environment. (Choose the best combination from the options below.)

(A) reactive...proactive

(B) proactive...reactive

(C) offensive...defensive

(D) defensive...offensive

(E) overt...covert

95. The simplest way to enter a foreign market is through

(A) joint venturing

(B) licensing

(C) management contracting

(D) direct investment

(E) exporting

96. Marketing a product in a foreign market without any change to the product is called

(A) straight extension

(B) product adaptation

(C) product invention

(D) communication adaptation

(E) dual adaptation

97. Which form of entry into a foreign market causes the most risk?

(A) Exporting

(B) Joint venturing

(C) Joint ownership

(D) Licensing

(E) Direct investment

98. Which type of joint venturing offers a low-risk method of getting into a foreign market and yields income from the beginning?

    (A) Licensing

    (B) Contract manufacturing

    (C) Management contracting

    (D) Joint ownership

    (E) Both (A) and (B) are correct.

99. With the high regulation of the U.S. government before the 1980s, carriers of products did not compete in which of these areas, as they do now?

    (A) Promotion

    (B) Price

    (C) Place

    (D) Product

    (E) Service

100. Sandy just bought a new Ford Taurus. Three weeks later, she received a rebate check for $300 in the mail. Which of the following forms of promotion was used in this example?

    (A) Advertising

    (B) Direct marketing

    (C) Sales promotion

    (D) Personal selling

    (E) Public relations

CLEP PRINCIPLES OF MARKETING
TEST 1

ANSWER KEY

1.	(B)	26.	(D)	51.	(A)	76.	(A)
2.	(C)	27.	(A)	52.	(C)	77.	(D)
3.	(D)	28.	(B)	53.	(C)	78.	(C)
4.	(A)	29.	(C)	54.	(B)	79.	(C)
5.	(D)	30.	(D)	55.	(B)	80.	(A)
6.	(B)	31.	(D)	56.	(A)	81.	(C)
7.	(B)	32.	(E)	57.	(B)	82.	(E)
8.	(E)	33.	(B)	58.	(C)	83.	(B)
9.	(A)	34.	(E)	59.	(A)	84.	(B)
10.	(C)	35.	(B)	60.	(E)	85.	(A)
11.	(C)	36.	(E)	61.	(E)	86.	(C)
12.	(D)	37.	(C)	62.	(B)	87.	(C)
13.	(B)	38.	(A)	63.	(B)	88.	(C)
14.	(C)	39.	(A)	64.	(A)	89.	(C)
15.	(B)	40.	(B)	65.	(A)	90.	(A)
16.	(E)	41.	(E)	66.	(C)	91.	(B)
17.	(D)	42.	(D)	67.	(B)	92.	(A)
18.	(D)	43.	(A)	68.	(D)	93.	(D)
19.	(D)	44.	(C)	69.	(E)	94.	(B)
20.	(C)	45.	(E)	70.	(B)	95.	(E)
21.	(E)	46.	(B)	71.	(E)	96.	(A)
22.	(A)	47.	(B)	72.	(D)	97.	(E)
23.	(A)	48.	(C)	73.	(C)	98.	(C)
24.	(E)	49.	(C)	74.	(D)	99.	(B)
25.	(C)	50.	(B)	75.	(E)	100.	(C)

DETAILED EXPLANATIONS OF ANSWERS

TEST 1

1.   **(B)**   The key word in the question is "production." Because production involves the making of the product, choice (B) is correct. Predicting the types of cars different people will buy (A), determining the features of the car (C), selling the car (D), and developing a sales promotion campaign for the car (E) are marketing activities and are therefore not correct answers.

2.   **(C)**   Macro-marketing looks at the marketing function in relation to society as a whole, while micro-marketing looks at activities of individual organizations. The dilemma occurs when marketing efforts of individual producers may not be good for society; therefore, (C) is the correct choice. Answers (A), (B), (D), (E), while partially correct statements, do not relate to society as a whole. Thus, they are not examples of the macro-micro dilemma.

3.   **(D)**   Marketing information systems help marketing managers with their decision making by making routine information available at the right time. Therefore, this is the correct choice. Decision support systems are computerized systems that help any decision maker, not just marketing managers (A). Time series analysis is a statistical forecasting tool (B), marketing research is helpful for solving non-routine problems (C), and consumer panels are groups of customers who help collect data (E).

4.   **(A)**   With an emphasis on selling more parts and outselling the competition, the company is run as if it were in the sales era. (A) is the correct choice. The production era (B) focused on the production of products. The marketing company era (C) is a time when companies embraced the marketing concept. The simple trade era (D) was when middlemen were introduced in the early role of marketing involving simple distribution. The marketing department era (E) tied together various marketing efforts under one department.

5.   **(D)**   The "four Ps" of a marketing mix are product, price, place, and promotion. These are the controllable variables a company applies in their marketing strategy. (D) is the correct choice. The remaining answers (A), (B), (C), and (E), while they contain portions of the marketing mix and elements important in marketing strategy, are not correct answers.

6.   **(B)**   Prices in a market-directed economic system vary to allocate resources and distribute income according to consumer preferences, so price is a rough measure of the value of resources used to produce goods and services. (B) is the correct answer. The remaining choices (A), (C), (D), and (E) relate to decisions that may be utilized in some pricing strategies and tactics but do not relate to the role of price at the macro-level of a market-directed economy, and are incorrect choices.

7.   **(B)**   Marketing applies to both for-profit and nonprofit organizations. Although a nonprofit's primary objective may not be to seek profit, the firm still wants to satisfy customer needs; consequently, the priorities will be different than a for-profit organization. The correct answer is (B). The remaining sentences about marketing are true. Marketing affects products and services that are bought (A) as well as product prices (D). Advertising and sales promotion are areas in the marketing mix (Promotion) (C) and marketing decisions would include how to sell products (E).

8.   **(E)**   In a pure subsistence economy, family units make all the products they consume; therefore, (E) is correct. In this type of economy, no marketing takes place because marketing doesn't occur unless two or more parties are willing to exchange something for something else, consequently, (A) is incorrect. In a planned economy, the government makes all decisions about the production and distribution of products and services; therefore, (C) is not the correct choice. In a pure subsistence economy, there is no need for middlemen, since marketing does not occur. (D) is not a correct choice.

9.   **(A)**   Tariffs are taxes on imported products therefore, (A) is the correct choice. Answer (B) describes "price-fixing," an action sometimes taken by companies which is considered illegal in the United States. Quotas are quantities of products that can be moved in or out of a country (C) and is not the correct answer. Extra money paid to officials for favored status is bribery and is illegal in the United States; therefore, (D) is not a correct answer. Tariffs are legal as long as all regulations are followed. (E) is not the correct answer.

10. **(C)** The question relates to a definition. Economies of scale means that as a company produces larger quantities of an item, the cost of producing each item goes down. (C) is the correct answer. Micro-marketing looks at marketing as a set of activities; (A) is incorrect. Possession utility is having the right to use a product; (B) is not correct. The marketing concept looks at satisfying customers needs. (D) is not correct. Transaction efficiency is not an "official" marketing term although it may be used to describe a process, thus, (E) is not correct.

11. **(C)** Along with the FCC guidelines, the Magnuson Act of 1975 ensures that warranties are clear and definite—not deceptive or unfair. The Act states that producers must provide a clearly written warranty; therefore, (C) is the correct choice. U.S. Common Law says (A) producers of goods must warrant their products as merchantable. Although it may reduce the responsibility of the firm (B), that was not the ruling of the Magnuson Act. The UPC code that identifies products with a readable electronic code was developed to speed the handling of fast-selling products (D). The Federal Fair Packaging and Labeling Act of 1966 required goods to be clearly labeled and understandable (E).

12. **(D)** When marketers compare their product to competitors' offerings, they are concerned with the quality and satisfaction of the total product (B, C). A SWOT analysis (A) is a comparison of a company's strengths vs. weaknesses, and opportunities vs. threats, rather than comparing single products. This eliminates (A) and (E) as possible correct answers.

13. **(B)** A deed performed by one party for another at a cost is a service. (B) is the correct choice. (A) Supplies are expense items that do not become a part of a finished product and are tangible. You cannot "hold" a service; therefore, (C) would be an incorrect answer. (A) is not the correct choice. A perishable good (D) is one that is subject to spoil, such as food. Consequently, (D) is not the correct choice. Because the correct answer is (B), choice (E) is not correct.

14. **(C)** Convenience products are products a customer needs but is not willing to shop around for; therefore, (C) is an incorrect choice, because when it comes to convenience products, customers DO NOT shop extensively. The three types of convenience products are staples, impulse products, and emergency products. Staples are products that are bought routinely without much thought. Therefore, (A) is a correct statement. If a

buyer does not see an impulse product at the right place, the sale will be lost. Therefore, (B) is a true statement, buyer behavior does affect place utility with impulse products. Because they are usually purchased in emergency situations, emergency products are purchased when urgently needed. (D) is a correct statement. (E) is also true. Branding does help customers cut shopping efforts and encourages repeat buying of satisfactory brands.

15. **(B)** In today's modern economy, market competition and product life cycles are changing at a fast pace. The product life cycle shows a firm needs different marketing mixes as a product moves through the cycle. It may no longer be profitable *just* to sell "me-too" products; firms need to expand their offerings; therefore, (B) is the correct choice. Most of the profits do not go to innovators (A), as profits rarely occur in the product introduction phase. Moreover, the failure rate of new products is high, not low (C), since only 2% of new products make it to market. The FTC ensures that products are safe for public use (D), but does not play a part in the planning of a new product. Since (A), (C), and (D) are incorrect choices, (E) would be eliminated as a correct answer.

16. **(E)** Customers pay for the capital items when they buy it, but for tax purposes the cost is spread over a number of years. Therefore, a long-lasting product that can be depreciated (D) is a capital item. An example of a capital item is an installation, buildings, land rights, or major equipment in any business or company (A); thus, (E) is the correct answer. Office supplies purchased by individuals are not long lasting, nor would a person depreciate office supplies over a number of years; therefore, (B) is not correct. Raw materials (C) are not considered capital items, but instead are expense items.

17. **(D)** All of the symbols are legally registered for the use of a single company. A trademark includes those words, symbols, or marks like (A), (B), and (C). By officially registering their seal, a company is protected legally from those who try to copy the label. Trademarks do not even need to be a word, they can be a symbol (C). (E) is incorrect because all the symbols are trademarks.

18. **(D)** This question relates to different levels of segmentation. Mass marketing (B) is the lowest level that doesn't involve any segmentation at all, and micro-marketing is the highest level of segmentation where firms try to offer products and services to suit individual customers' needs

(D). Niche marketing (A) caters to segments within segments of customers. Segment marketing (C) offers different products for different groups of customers (not at the individual level). Macro-marketing deals with marketing at the societal level and is clearly inappropriate in this situation.

19. **(D)**   By meeting customers needs better, a better package can help create a "new" product for a "new" market. The packaging of a product (A) does not provide better shelf placement. Consumer demand and extra money paid for shelf space dictate the shelf placement of a product. The average packaging costs are between 1 and 70% rather than over 95% (B). The Federal Packaging and Labeling Act (C) does not hold restrictions on packaging—rather its various laws provide general guidance on packaging issues and the producers can choose whether or not to abide by them. If consumers do not understand the terminology, labeling can become misleading, but the statement that labels are inaccurate and no one reads them (E) is not true. Many labels are correct and many people do read labels.

20. **(C)**   Brand nonrecognition means that final consumers do not recognize a brand at all. (C) is the correct answer. Brand rejection (A) occurs when a customer refuses to buy a certain brand. Brand recognition (B) happens when customers remember the brands they buy. Brand preference (D) means that customers choose one brand over other brands, perhaps out of habit. Brand insistence (E) occurs when customers insist on a firm's branded products and are willing to search for it by any means. Hence, the example in the question clearly demonstrates a customer who is exhibiting brand nonrecognition (C).

21. **(E)**   Shopping products the customer sees as basically the same are homogeneous—customers do not think the brand differences are important, they just look at the price. (E) is the correct answer. Specialty products (A) are those that the customer really wants and makes a special effort to find—it does not involve comparing prices or brands. Convenience products (C) are those that a customer needs but is not willing to spend much time shopping for—often bought on an impulse, no comparing is used here either. Regularly sought products (D) is not a division of product class. This term may be confused with regularly unsought products, which are a division of product class.

22. **(A)**   Geographical segmentation involves customizing products and services for groups of customers based on where they reside. That is

what Progresso Soup seems to be doing in this question. Therefore, the correct answer is (A). Behavioral segmentation (B) is done based on usage behavior. That is not what the question describes. Similarly, demographic (C) and psychographic segmentation (D) can be ruled out since the former deals with users' demographics such as age, occupation, and income while the latter deals with customers' lifestyles. There is no such thing as political segmentation (E), so that can be eliminated.

23. **(A)** is the correct answer because it is the only statement that is entirely not true. Just because industry sales rise doesn't mean that industry profits will also rise. Increased competition among individual companies within the industry could prompt lower selling prices in the industry which would lead to lower profits for the industry. Increased sales could also prompt expensive investments in capital equipment which would decrease profits if the individual firms are already operating at full capacity. (B) is not the correct answer because the statement is true. Customers' attitudes as well as needs will change over time. Thus, a customer who bought the product in the past may no longer have need for the product, or a customer who previously didn't have a need for the product may acquire a need for the product (target markets may change). (C) is also not correct because the statement is true. Once a product proves its profit potential, everybody will want to sell the product to get a piece of the "profit pie." (D) is also incorrect because the statement is true. Growth refers to sales growth, not necessarily profit growth. Remember, competition enters in this stage, which, in general, tends to decrease profits. (E) is also not correct because although (D) is true, (A) is not true.

24. **(E)** is correct because all of the statements are correct. Industry profits initially do increase (A), but later industry profits start to decline (B). Also, more companies enter the industry because they see that industry profits initially are increasing (C). Furthermore, industry sales increase (D) because of heightened consumer awareness. (A), (B), (C), and (D) are all correct; consequently, (E) is the correct answer.

25. **(C)** Occupation (C) is a demographic segmentation variable and is the correct choice. Social class (A), personality (B), lifestyle (D), and interests (E) are all psychographic segmentation variables.

26. **(D)** The four major categories or bases for segmentation are geographic (A), demographic (B), behavioral (C), and psychographic (E). Therefore, the correct answer is moods (D), which is not one of the four bases noted.

27. **(A)** The demand is elastic. Any increase in price that creates a decrease in total revenue is said to be elastic. (B) is not correct, because in order for the demand to be inelastic, the total revenue would have to have increased. Unitary elasticity (C) occurs when the total revenue stays the same when the price of a product is changed. There is not enough information given to know whether or not the meat is old (D). Elasticity can be determined from the information given, so (E) is incorrect.

28. **(B)** is the correct answer, the demand is elastic. When a firm or organization reduces their price and total revenues increase (or stretch), the demand is said to be elastic. (A) is incorrect. In order for the demand to be unitarily elastic, the revenue would have to stay the same. Inelasticity would occur if the total revenue decreased in conjunction with a decrease in price (C). (D) and (E) are both incorrect. You cannot have elasticity and inelasticity at the same time, and in the example, revenue of the Yearous Group showed an increase, while the price was dropped.

29. **(C)** is the correct answer. The farmer's crop would most likely be elastic. If the farmer dropped his price, more people would buy his potatoes. Potatoes are a commodity where people shop for the "best buy." (A) is incorrect because the total revenue would, in all likelihood, increase, not decrease, with a price reduction. (B) is incorrect because people shopping for potatoes are price conscious and shop for the least expensive. (D) is incorrect because the total revenue would not stay the same with an increase or decrease in price for this type of product. (E) cannot be true because demand must be elastic, inelastic, or have unitary elasticity.

30. **(D)** Bob would find himself in a situation with unitary elasticity. When raising or lowering the price of your product has no effect on total revenue, the situation is said to have unitary elasticity of demand. (A) is wrong because Bob can make a conclusion about demand. (B) is also incorrect because if the demand were elastic, when the price was dropped, total revenues would increase, and when the price was raised, total revenues would decrease. (C) is also wrong because if it were inelastic, when Bob tried to lower his price, he would find that his total revenue would also be lower, yet if he raised his price, his total revenue would increase. With the information given, we don't know whether he should sell shrimp (E).

31. **(D)** The standard commission used in advertising agencies is 15% of media billing. In this question, 15% of $20,000 is $3,000. Therefore, (D) is the right answer.

32. **(E)** All the answers are examples of retailing. Retailing refers to the selling of products and services to the final consumer. (E) is correct. (A) is a good example of retailing at a college level, with the final consumer being the faculty at the college. (B) is also a type of retailing, although not a pleasant one for the car owner. (C) is door-to-door retailing involving selling a product to a final consumer. (D) is probably the most common type of retailing, where the final consumer goes directly to the point-of-sale for a product.

33. **(B)** The rate of usage, i.e., light, medium, or heavy, is an example of usage behavior and is part of the behavioral segmentation category (B). Geographic segmentation deals with where people reside (A), demographic segmentation is dividing a market based on factors such as age, income, gender, and occupation (C). Psychographic segmentation breaks down a market based on users' lifestyles (D). Geodemographic segmentation (E) is also incorrect because it is a combination of answers (A) and (C).

34. **(E)** Positioning is giving a product a specific image that differentiates it from its competition (A), and this is done to occupy a certain place in consumers' minds in relation to competing brands (B). Since both (A) and (B) are true statements, the correct answer is (E). Positioning is as important as segmentation, so (C) is incorrect. Also, positioning can be used by any firm regardless of size or status, so (D) too is incorrect.

35. **(B)** is correct because pleasing products are not good for consumers' in the long run but do give immediate satisfaction. Disposable diapers satisfy the parents' need for convenience but are not good for the environment and thus are not good for consumers in the long run. (A) is not correct because a desirable product gives immediate satisfaction and is good for consumers in the long run. (C) is not correct because performance products are not a type of new product opportunity. (D) is not correct because deficient products do not satisfy consumers in the long run or provide immediate satisfaction. (E) is not correct because salutary products are good for consumers in the long run but do not give the consumer immediate satisfaction.

36. **(E)** is the correct answer because industry sales do level off in market maturity (A). Profits can increase for a particular company if they have a marketing mix that appeals to consumers (B). (C) is correct because some firms are not efficiently using their product and thus can't

compete in the price wars of their more efficient competitors, so they drop out of the industry. Promotion costs rise (D) because firms want to promote their product as different, or they want to remind consumers about the product and its uses to keep sales from falling.

37.　**(C)**　The American cowboy is a cultural icon used by Stetson in its advertising to reinforce its American roots. Therefore, (C) is the right choice. Stetson's positioning is not based on a particular feature of the product, so (A) is incorrect. It is also not based on Stetson's user profile (B). (D) is incorrect because the question makes no reference to Stetson's competition. Finally, since the question doesn't indicate a tangible product benefit, (E) is incorrect.

38.　**(A)**　This is a question of evaluating which type of buying method is being used in the process of purchasing a product for this company. The descriptive buying method is a form of buying a product through a written or verbal description and is often done without inspection. This purchase is usually based on a mutual trust between buyers and sellers and is used to reduce the cost of buying; (A) is the correct choice. There is no such thing as test buying, although it does sound good, so (B) is an invalid answer. Inspection buying is the process of inspecting every item before you buy it; (C) is not the best choice. Sampling buying means looking at only part of the potential purchase, making the assumption that the whole purchase will be of the same standards; (D) is not correct. Negotiated contract buying means agreeing to a contract to purchase, but the contract allows for changes in the purchasing arrangements; (E) is an incorrect choice.

39.　**(A)**　The Multiple Buying Influence means several people—perhaps even top management—share in making a purchase decision. Because the question pertains to a business, the general public would not influence the decision to purchase a copier. (A) is the correct choice. The next four choices are all part of the Multiple Buying Influence. An influencer (B) could be an engineer or research person who helps to write specifications or supply information for evaluating alternatives. A buyer (C) could be a purchasing agent who has the responsibility for working with suppliers and arranging terms of the sale. Deciders (D) are people in the organization who have the power to select or approve the supplier. A gatekeeper (E) is a person who controls the information throughout the whole organization.

40. **(B)**   The business exchange function in a market driven society involves giving an object or service to someone in exchange for money. Money is the price. (A) is incorrect because it is a starting point for price negotiation. Many times wholesalers and retailers are willing to change the "Price" in exchange for quantity purchases, to get rid of out-of-season merchandise, and many other reasons. Price is not calculated by dividing cost by selling price; thus, (C) is incorrect. Cost is how much the product or service "costs," or is paid for, by the intermediary or manufacturer. Adding a markup to that figure gives a price; thus, (D) is not correct. And (E) is not correct because price may be driven by something other than profit, such as sales.

41. **(E)**   is the correct choice. The shirt would be marked up $600. To calculate the amount of markup, you use the formula Amount of Markup = Selling Price – Cost. If the shirt sold for $1,000, and the cost to Sally was $400, then $1,000 – $400 = $600. (A), (B), (C), and (D) are incorrect.

42. **(D)**   is the correct answer. Percent markup based upon the selling price is calculated by dividing the selling, or retail, price into the amount of the markup. (A) is incorrect because 600/1,000 = 60%, not 10%. Likewise, (B) and (C) are incorrect. Amount of Markup/Selling Price = Percent Markup, thus the answer can be determined, and (E) is incorrect.

43. **(A)**   is the correct choice. If the cost of a product is $400, and the markup percent on the retail selling price is 60%, then, by formula, the selling price is $1,000. The calculation can be made by taking the cost of the product and dividing it by 1 minus the percent of selling price. Thus, (B), (C), (D), and (E) are incorrect. $400/1 – .60 = $1,000.

44. **(C)**   is the correct answer. In order to calculate the maximum cost, use the following formula: Cost + Markup = Retail Sales Price.

$$x + (.40)x = 3$$
$$1.4x = 3$$
$$x = 2.14$$

The maximum Ron and Dee can pay per tile is $2.14. Thus, answers (A), (B), and (D) are incorrect. (E) is incorrect because the answer can be determined based on the information provided.

45. **(E)**   is the correct answer. If Pake Productions utilizes the new price for the speakers, $160, then their markdown would be 25%. If they

utilize the original price as the denominator, then the markdown percentage is 20%. (A) and (B) are both incorrect as they are dollar amounts, not percentages. While 25% (C) is a good answer for calculating the markdown percentage on the new selling price (Amount of Markdown/New Sales Price, or $40/$160), it is not the most correct. Likewise with (D); if Pake calculated the markdown on the original price ($40/$200), this would be the correct answer, although it is not the correct answer for the question. The markdown calculation depends on the accounting system being used. Both markdown methods are common.

46. **(B)** is the correct choice. The terms on an invoice 2/10 net 30, indicate that the buyers will get a two percent discount if they pay the bill early. This is to increase the amount of cash flow for the seller and to encourage early payment of bills. (A) is not the correct choice. If Ogden & Ogden had paid the bill after the ten-day period, this would have been the amount they owed. (C) is also incorrect. However, if Ogden & Ogden had paid the bill after the 30-day net, they may have owed this interest, depending on the payment terms agreed upon between the buyer and seller. (D) and (E) are simply not correct. The Ogden & Ogden Company would not have paid that amount based upon the terms of the invoice.

47. **(B)** Place is the correct answer. By definition, Promotion (A) is communicating information between the seller and potential buyers. Product (C) is the need satisfying offering of a firm. Price (D) is what is charged for something. Consequently, making goods and services available in the right quantities and locations describes Place (B), the correct choice; and (E) is therefore not correct.

48. **(C)** A channel of distribution is any series of firms or individuals who participate in the flow of goods from producer to final user; therefore, (C) is the correct choice. Regrouping activities (A) adjust the quantities and assortments of products handled. Accumulating (B) involves collecting products from many small producers. Bulk-breaking (D) involves dividing larger quantities into smaller quantities. Because (C) is the correct choice, (E) would be incorrect.

49. **(C)** Direct mail (C) is the second largest category of expense after telemarketing in the direct marketing industry.

50. **(B)** One of the biggest advantages of direct marketing is that firms can tailor their campaign to fit the needs of individual customers

(B). Low cost (A) is not necessarily a strong suit of direct marketing, although if done correctly, it is economical only because it is so targeted at specific customers. Both (C) and (D) are incorrect because fast response time cannot be taken for granted (C) and the ability to use J.I.T. is not contingent upon using direct marketing. (E) is incorrect since direct marketing has a low rate of consumer acceptance.

51. **(A)**   Selective distribution occurs when a company only sells through middlemen who will give the product special attention; consequently, (A) is the correct answer. Intensive distribution (B) occurs when a company sells a product through all responsible and suitable retailers who will stock and sell the product. Exclusive distribution (C) occurs when a company sells through only one middleman in a particular geographic area. Ideal market exposure (D) makes a product available widely enough to satisfy target customer's needs. Because (A) is the correct choice, (E) cannot be correct.

52. **(C)**   A PR "hit" is defined as the number of times a company's name is mentioned in a particular news story (C). PR firms are often evaluated based on the number of "hits" they obtain on behalf of their clients. None of the other choices correctly defines a PR "hit."

53. **(C)**   Dual distribution occurs when a producer uses several competing channels to reach the same target market; (C) is the correct answer. Exclusive distribution (A) means that a company sells through only one middleman or one channel. Intensive distribution (B) means selling products through all responsible and suitable sellers. Since (A) and (B) are both incorrect, (D) would not be correct. (E) would also be an incorrect answer because (C) is correct.

54. **(B)**   Dual distribution occurs when a producer uses several competing channels to reach the same target market. One reason this occurs is that retailers want large quantities with a lower price per unit; (B) is the best choice. Dual distribution is not needed for convenience products and business suppliers. These types of products are best served by intensive distribution because customers want these products available everywhere. One of the reasons a producer moves toward dual distribution is that current channel members are doing a poor job, so (C) is not a correct answer. (D) is not correct because both (A) and (C) are incorrect and, therefore, (E) cannot be correct either.

55. **(B)**   A company newsletter (B) is meant for employees of that firm and is therefore an internal communication device. None of the other choices is truly "internal" since their audiences include "external" stakeholders.

56. **(A)**   Horizontal and vertical conflicts are the two basic types of conflicts in channels of distribution. Horizontal conflicts occur between firms at the same level in the channel of distribution. Vertical conflicts occur between firms at different levels of the channel of distribution. (A) is the correct answer. Discrepancy of quantity (B) means the difference between the quantity of products it is economical for a producer to make and the quantity final users or consumers want. Discrepancy of assortment means the difference between the lines a typical producer makes and the assortment final consumers or users want. Assorting (C) means putting together a variety of products, and sorting means separating products into grades. (D) is not a correct choice because both (B) and (C) are incorrect, and (E) is not correct because (A) is the correct answer.

57. **(B)**   is the correct choice. Services included are on-time delivery, quality control, custom design, nationwide distribution systems, along with technical advice. (A) is incorrect because prices are often elastic, requiring the firm to price at or near the prices of their competitors. This keeps prices stable. (C) is also incorrect. Industrial marketing is unique for environmental services, but is not the MOST emphasized area. The distribution emphasis is just to make sure products are available, so (D) is not the correct answer. And even though there is an element of sales promotion in an industrial setting, this is not the most emphasized element of the industrial mix; thus, (E) is incorrect.

58. **(C)**   The example shows administered pricing, so (C) is the correct choice. In administered pricing, the seller sets the price and the buyer pays that listed price. If a price is determined through the use of sealed or open bids, it is called bid pricing. Thus, (A) is incorrect. In negotiated pricing, there is a stated list price; however, discounting is used to entice purchases. (B) is therefore incorrect. This is not a retail situation, so retail pricing is an incorrect answer (D). In economic pricing (E), the business environment has more of an impact on the price set than the seller, so this is a wrong choice.

59. **(A)**   A perceptual map is a two-dimensional diagram that depicts a brand's "position" along two product attributes in relation to its competi-

tion. Therefore, (A) is the correct answer. The perceptual map has very little to do with either product design (B) or packaging (C). (D) and (E) imply geographical maps and thus are incorrect.

60. **(E)** Advertising can make customers aware of all of these areas; thus, (E) is the correct answer. Advertisements allow customers to become aware of new products or brands that they may not otherwise be aware of (A). Additionally, advertising allows the customer to become exposed to product features (B). Advertising can expose potential customers to organizations (C) and customer representatives (D). In summary, advertising is used to reach customers for all of the reasons listed in the answers.

61. **(E)** All of the statements are true; therefore, (E) is the correct answer. Marketing strategy can help develop flexibility in providing additional customer service, so (A) is incorrect. Marketing strategy provides a road map, giving the marketers a direction and showing what types of expertise are needed, thus facilitating the hiring of high-quality personnel (B), so this answer is not correct. Effective strategy planning is proactive in giving solutions to potential problems, thus (C) is also not true. An effective marketing strategy plan can provide for the utilization of high technology to decrease overall service costs to customers, so (D) is also not true.

62. **(B)** Marketing activities undertaken by groups without an objective of profit, ROI, or market share are called nonbusiness marketing activities. An example of such an activity may be a beer manufacturer running an ad campaign to reduce teenage drinking. (A) is incorrect because they are not, or should not, be a waste of time. They may be providing useful information to the listener or viewer. (C) is incorrect; although they may be strategic in nature, the purpose is nonbusiness. Promotional marketing activities (D) refer to activities and processes undertaken as a part of the promotional mix (i.e., advertising, public relations, sales promotion, selling) and is incorrect. Nonmarketing activities (E) is incorrect, because these are marketing functions and activities.

63. **(B)** Salespersons are classified as being order getters, order takers, or missionaries. A department store salesperson who performs a cashier's role is essentially involved in taking orders (B) from customers. The salesperson is not actively soliciting orders (A) nor is that person helping other sales personnel complete an order (D). A PR specialist is far removed from any sales-oriented task, so (C) is incorrect. A copywriter is one who writes copy for advertisements, so (E) too is incorrect.

64. **(A)** TQM (Total Quality Management) describes how companies can use quality to create value and enhance customer satisfaction. This is the perfect choice for the question since it applies in all situations (A). Low prices (B), manufacturing superiority (C), celebrity advertising (D), and sales promotions (E) represent just part of the solution toward creating value and customer satisfaction. They are not sufficient by themselves. Therefore, they are incorrect answers.

65. **(A)** Although many people think money is very important, it is not a level in the hierarchy of needs. (A) is the correct choice. Safety needs (B) are concerns about personal protection and well-being and are a level in the hierarchy of needs. Physiological needs (C) are needs for food, drink, rest, and sex and are a level in the hierarchy of needs. Social needs (D) are needs for love, friendship, status, esteem, and acceptance by others and are also a level in the hierarchy of needs. Since (A) is the answer, (E) would be an incorrect choice.

66. **(C)** The definition of learning is a change in a person's thought processes caused by prior experience; therefore, (C) is the correct answer. A cue (A) is a product sign, ad, or other stimuli in the environment. Responses (B) are efforts to satisfy a strong stimulus that encourages action. A belief (D) is a person's opinion about something. Reinforcement (E) occurs when a response is followed by satisfaction. Cue, response, belief, and reinforcement all occur during the learning process.

67. **(B)** In psychographics or lifestyle analysis, marketers use AIO to analyze people's day-to-day patterns of behavior. A stands for Activities, I stands for Interests, and O stands for opinions, making (B) the correct choice. Any other combinations as in (A), (C), (D), and (E) would be incorrect choices.

68. **(D)** The current trend in business is target marketing whereby they have to clearly define their target market and then try to customize an offer for them. The mass-marketing model no longer holds good given the tremendous diversity of customer needs. Therefore, (D) is the right answer. Target marketing (A), segmentation (B), and positioning (C) are all geared toward the current trend in marketing management. Direct marketing (E) is growing and is therefore incorrect.

69. **(E)** Positioning is defined as the process of creating a favorable image of your brand in relation to competing brands. Therefore, (E) is the

correct answer. Mass marketing (A) is marketing to everyone with a standardized offering, not just target customers. Target marketing (B) and segmentation (C) deal with breaking up a heterogeneous market into smaller and distinct homogeneous submarkets. Green marketing (D) is environmentally friendly marketing.

70. **(B)** Extensive problem-solving occurs for a completely new or important need involving high involvement in how to satisfy it. The best answer is a washing machine (B), because there is typically high involvement in such a major purchase. Milk (A) and toilet paper (D) purchases are routinized behaviors requiring little involvement. Buying a pair of shoes (C) and T-shirts (E) involve limited problem-solving.

71. **(E)** The adoption process comprises the steps people go through on the journey of accepting or rejecting a new idea. Payment (E) is not one of these steps. The six steps are as follows: Awareness (C), Interest, Evaluation, Trial (B), Decision (D), and Confirmation (A).

72. **(D)** New product development deals with developing ideas for new products and is not a function of channels of distribution; therefore, (D) is the correct answer. Alleviating discrepancies in assortment (A) and in quantity (B) are both function of distribution channels. Because providing customer service is integrated in all aspects of marketing, (C) is also a function. Creating channels of distribution create time, place, and possession utility, so (E) is also a function of distribution.

73. **(C)** Transforming is not used as a regrouping activity by channel specialists; therefore, (C) is the correct choice. Regrouping activities adjust the quantities and assortments of products handled. Assorting (A) means putting together a variety of products. Accumulating (B) involves collecting products from many small producers. Bulk-breaking (D) involves dividing larger quantities into smaller quantities. Sorting (E) means separating products into grades and qualities desired by the target market.

74. **(D)** In a complex selling situation that calls for high levels of persuasion, personal selling is often thought to be more effective than advertising primarily because of the direct interaction between the buyer and seller. Thus, (D) is the right answer. Personal selling is one of the most expensive methods of promotion on a per contact basis, so (A) is incorrect. In a given time period, advertising can reach a lot more people than personal selling. Thus, (B) is incorrect. Personal selling is much more

effective when the demand is elastic because that is when the demand changes substantially in response to changes in price. So, (C) is incorrect. (E) is also incorrect since (A) and (B) are false.

75. **(E)** Vertical channel integration is the combining of two or more stages of the channel under one management. (E) is the best answer. A strategic alliance (A) is a partnership formed to create a competitive advantage on a worldwide bases. Horizontal channel integration (B) deals with combining institutions at the same level of operation. Reverse channels (C) are used to retrieve products that consumers no longer want. An oligopoly (D) is a competitive structure existing when a few sellers control the supply of a large proportion of a product.

76. **(A)** The best type of distribution for this scenario would be intensive distribution, because sellers want the product to be easily reached by everyone. Exclusive distribution (B) is using a single outlet and would not answer the request for availability. Vertical distribution (C) and horizontal distribution (D) are not types of distribution. Selective distribution (E) means using only some available outlets to distribute a product, which also would not satisfy the availability factor.

77. **(D)** The definition of exclusive distribution is using a single outlet in a fairly large geographic area to distribute a product or service; therefore, (D) is the correct answer. Exclusive distribution also creates the "mystique" marketers want to make the product more appealing. Selective distribution (A) is used when you want middlemen to give a product special attention. Selective distribution uses many outlets to distribute the product but not as many as intensive. Universal distribution (B) would not be correct because it is not a distribution classification. Intensive distribution (C) would not be correct because sellers do want the product to be easily reached by everyone. In exclusive distribution, sellers only want the product to be available to those who can afford the product.

78. **(C)** E-commerce has been plagued by concerns about security and identity theft (C). Although advances in encryption technology have alleviated some of these fears, it is still the biggest deterrent to sales among the choices outlined in this question. None of the other choices correctly identifies a major concern of e-commerce.

79. **(C)** Exclusive dealing forbids an intermediary to carry products of a competing manufacturer. A tying agreement (A) requires a channel

member to buy other products from a supplier besides the one preferred by the channel member. A monopoly (B) involves a market structure that exists when an organization produces a product that has no close substitutes and becomes the sole source of supply. A strategic channel alliance (D) is a marketing channel that exists when the products of one organization are distributed through the marketing channels of another organization. A vertical marketing system (E) occurs when channel activities are coordinated by a single channel member to achieve efficient, low-cost distribution aimed at satisfying the target market.

80.   **(A)**   A coupon for a bag of chips on a bottle of Pepsi is an example of a cross promotion that is specifically referred to as a "cross-ruff coupon" (A). In this case, Pepsi has a tie-in agreement with the firm that is marketing the potato chips so that both companies benefit from this cross promotion. None of the other terms correctly describes this promotional offer by Pepsi.

81.   **(C)**   Most contemporary brands are positioned in consumers' minds with respect to their features. For instance, Dell tries to position its computer as being "easy-to-use." Therefore, (C) is the best choice. Although all the other options, which includes against a competitor (A), away from a competitor (B), user's lifestyle (D), and user's occupation (E), are valid positioning characteristics, they are relatively less popular compared to product attributes.

82.   **(E)**   The three "pillars" of the marketing concept are customer satisfaction, team effort, and the firm's objective. In this question, only customer satisfaction (E) appears as one of the choices. None of the other choices are in the marketing concept and, therefore, are incorrect.

83.   **(B)**   When a company chooses one attribute to excel at and promotes it to create a competitive advantage, it is called a unique selling proposition. Thus, (B) is the right answer. There is no such thing as overpositioning (A). Undifferentiated marketing (C) is when a company chooses to mass market its product or service. Relationship marketing (D) is when companies aim to create lasting relationships with its stakeholders. Concentrated marketing (E) is also incorrect because it is a segmentation strategy where companies target one segment to pursue with a unique marketing mix.

84.   **(B)**   E-commerce and other Internet-based firms prefer flexible and dynamic pricing policies (B) compared to the other choices that are more restrictive in nature.

85.   **(A)**   This question deals with brand sponsor decisions. Manufacturers' brands, such as Heinz ketchup, dominate the American scene. Many manufacturers create their own brand and some even rent well-known brand names by paying royalties. Choices (B), (C), and (D) are all private brands owned by Sears. Sears (a retailer) does not produce many of the products that carry its name, but instead contracts with manufacturers to produce these products on the chain's behalf. Thus, these are incorrect choices. Because (A) is the best answer, (E) cannot be correct.

86.   **(C)**   This question deals with the broad topic of brand decisions. A company may be able to use any one of these decisions for its products. The strategy described in this question relates to the multibrand decision, so (C) is the correct answer. Brand repositioning (A) may be needed if a competitor launched a brand that competes directly with an existing product. Brand extension decisions (B) relate to any effort to use a successful brand name to launch product modifications or new products. Family brands (D) are created by manufacturers who brand their products. Brand quality (E) supports the brand decision in the target market.

87.   **(C)**   Setting low prices is consistent with penetration pricing and current profit maximization. Therefore, (C) is the logical answer. Low prices do not always translate into higher market share. Thus, (A) is incorrect. Similarly, low prices do not guarantee superior product quality (B) or survival in the market (D). Just-in-time is an inventory management tool that has very little to do with low prices; thus, (E) is also incorrect.

88.   **(C)**   The basic difference between fixed and variable costs is that fixed costs do not change with the volume of output, while variable costs do. Rent, heating bills, air-conditioning costs, interest payments, and executive salaries are all expenses that do not change with the level of output. So, they are fixed costs and the correct answer is (C). There is no such thing as monopoly costs (E) or independent costs (D). They are also not standard costs (A) or variable costs (B).

89.   **(C)**   This question pertains to a company's product line-stretching decisions. Line stretching occurs when a company lengthens its product line beyond its current range. A company may stretch downward for

any of the above reasons except (C). Therefore, (C) is the correct answer. When a company decides to stretch upward, it may be because the company at the lower end of the market may want to enter the higher end (C).

90. **(A)**   Globalization has resulted in a big surge in competition both in the U.S. market and overseas. Because of increasing competition, more and more companies are consolidating their promotion activities in the form of Integrated Marketing Communications. Therefore, (A) is the correct choice. Advertising costs are on the rise, so (B) is untrue. There is no evidence that sales promotion is on the decline (C) or that costs of personal selling have gone up across the board (D). Since IMC may use many different kinds of media, (E) is incorrect.

91. **(B)**   This is a definitional question since only single-source data systems allow managers to link TV advertising to store choice behavior (B). Motivational research is a type of qualitative marketing research that seeks in-depth answers from respondents (A). The Peoplemeter is used by A.C. Nielsen to measure TV ratings (C). Subliminal research is also irrelevant here since it involves subliminal perception (D). Focus groups are also a qualitative research method (E).

92. **(A)**   is the right choice because the industrial structure shapes a country's product and service needs, income, and employment levels. The income distribution determines if the income of the population in that country would create a market for the product. These things are economically important. Political stability and attitudes (B) and cultural environment and government bureaucracy (C) are not really economic factors that reflect the country's attractiveness. Rather, they are factors that are involved in the political-legal attractiveness of the country environmentally. (D) and (E) do not deal with why one does business in a foreign country; they are actually dealing with *how* one does business.

93. **(D)**   is correct. An industrializing economy needs more imports of certain products as manufacturing increases. A subsistence economy (A) offers few market opportunities and a rich class seldom exists. A raw-material-exporting economy (B) gains much of their revenues from exporting one particular natural resource; therefore, their economy has either a poor class or wealthy upper class. An industrialized economy (C) has varied manufacturing activities and a large middle class. Answer (E) is incorrect because one of the above is indeed true.

94. **(B)**   Marketers could either try to actively manage the environment (proactive) or merely react to changes later (reactive). Successful companies always choose the former rather than the latter. Therefore, (B) is the best choice. None of the other choices can be generalized to *all* successful companies.

95. **(E)**   Exporting is the simplest way to enter a foreign market because all of the goods are manufactured or produced in the home country. In joint venturing (A), the company has to join with a partner to set up production facilities abroad which help to complicate entry, and dilute control. Licensing (B) and management contracting (C) are methods, or types, of joint venturing and are not correct. Direct investment (D) has the biggest involvement because the company develops foreign-based assembly or manufacturing facilities. This makes the entry into the foreign market much more difficult, not simple.

96. **(A)**   is correct. Straight extension is the only strategy for marketing a product in a foreign market without any product changes. Product adaptation (B) by definition involves changing the product to meet the local conditions. Certain aspects of the product such as packaging, branding, or labeling can be changed. Product invention (C) consists of creating something new. Both communication adaptation (D) and dual adaptation (E) are promotional strategies, not product strategies, and are incorrect choices.

97. **(E)**   Direct investment involves the highest risk (E). Direct investment risks include devalued currencies, falling markets, and government takeover (nationalization). Exporting (A) involves very little risk because the company can passively export surpluses from time to time, or it can actively commit to the country. While joint venturing (B) often gives a company less control, it doesn't involve as much risk as direct investment. Joint ownership (C) is a type of joint venturing, and is incorrect. Licensing (D) is also a type of joint venturing, so it is incorrect.

98. **(C)**   Management contracting is the best answer because the domestic firm is exporting services rather than products. With licensing (A), the company may give up not only potential profits, but it could also create a competitor when the contract ends. Contract manufacturing (B) provides less control over the manufacturing process and a loss of potential profits. Joint ownership (D) provides the risk that the partners could disagree over issues such as investment and marketing strategies. (E) is incorrect since both (A) and (B) are not correct answers.

99.   **(B)**   Before the 1980s, regulation of the country's transportation systems was intense. The federal government set the rates that could be charged by the carriers. Therefore, carriers could not compete on price as they do now. The carriers had to compete with the other variables of the marketing mix, and often had increases in promotion (A). The government did not tell the carriers where to ship (C), so that is incorrect. Product offerings (D) and service offerings (E) are also incorrect because the carriers were competing in these areas to make up for the lack of differences in cost.

100.   **(C)**   Rebates are a common form of sales promotion similar to coupons, sweepstakes, and special sales offers that offer temporary incentives to customers to try a product. Therefore, (C) is the right answer. Advertising is a form of mass communication aimed at a large audience, so (A) is incorrect. Direct marketing involves a direct communication between the buyer and seller usually involving an immediate response, so (B) is incorrect. Personal selling involves a direct face-to-face interaction between the buyer and seller, so (D) is incorrect. Public relations (E) is also incorrect since rebate offers do not constitute publicity for a firm.

PRACTICE
TEST 2

CLEP PRINCIPLES OF MARKETING
Test 2

(Answer sheets appear in the back of this book.)

TIME: 90 Minutes
100 Questions

DIRECTIONS: Each of the questions or incomplete statements below is followed by five possible answers or completions. Select the best choice in each case and fill in the corresponding oval on the answer sheet.

---

1. Based upon retail selling price, if John Doe wants to figure out the actual amount of markup of a product he plans to retail, he should

    (A) divide the selling price by the cost

    (B) divide the cost by the selling price

    (C) subtract the cost from the selling price

    (D) subtract the cost from the markup

    (E) Cannot be determined from the information given

2. With a selling price of $2,000 and a cost of $800, what would the markup (at retail) be for this product?

    (A) $1,000   (D) $800

    (B) $2,000   (E) $1,250

    (C) $1,200

3. Joe Fisherman wants to know his percent markup on retail of a pair of shoes for which he paid $1,000. He knows the amount of markup was $600. Which of the following would answer his question?

(A) 40%
(D) 60%

(B) 150%
(E) 100%

(C) 50%

4.   The MOLE, a toy retailer, wants to calculate the selling price for some of their stuffed dolls. They know that they paid $400 each for the dolls, and they want a 60% markup on selling price. What should their selling price be?

(A) $640
(D) $1,000

(B) $350
(E) $5,300

(C) $750

5.   Jan and Bob Winfield want to calculate the cost of a new chair they just bought. Jan told Bob that the retail selling price of the chair was $1,000, and that the markup percent on the selling price was 60%. What would their cost be?

(A) $1,000
(D) $400

(B) $600
(E) $150

(C) $625

6.   The McHenry Store, a retailer of fine clothing, wants to calculate both the cost and selling price of a new suit they received from a fine clothing tailor. The amount of markup on selling price is 20%, and the amount of markup is $100. Can they calculate both the cost and the selling price of the product?

(A) Definitely not; they must have more information.

(B) Certainly; the selling price is $500 and the cost is $400.

(C) Certainly; the selling price is $1,000 and the cost is $400.

(D) Of course they can; the selling price is $500 and the cost is $200.

(E) Yes; the cost is $100 and the selling price is $120.

7.   When trying to calculate markup based on product cost, Doc and Den wanted to determine the markup on a product that cost $150 and sold for $200. What is their markup?

(A) $25   (D) $60

(B) $40   (E) $110

(C) $50

8.   Which of the following is a marketing management tool that shows how customers perceive proposed and/or present brands?

(A) Market segmentation   (D) Brand equity

(B) Diversification   (E) Positioning

(C) Market penetration

9.   Judy and Dale want to calculate the selling price (on COST) of an item that has a cost of $10.00 and a markup percent on cost of 40%. What is their selling price?

(A) $16.67   (D) $12.00

(B) $10.00   (E) $14.00

(C) $10.50

10. Which of the following statements about positioning is FALSE? Positioning techniques

(A) require a firm to collect data about consumer perceptions of products

(B) are sometimes called perceptual mapping techniques

(C) typically rely on a "product space" diagram to show the relationship among competing products

(D) may use information on consumers' "ideal products" so that the preferences of different consumer segments can be considered

(E) place products on a graph based on price level and quantity demanded

11. When entering a foreign market, a marketer may need to adapt or modify which of the following promotional methods to meet the culture norms of the target market?

(A) Theme   (D) Media

(B) Copy color   (E) All of the above

(C) Product's name

12. When preparing to market internationally, what is the typical chronological progression (or order) that most companies would follow?

    (A) Export department; international division; multinational organization

    (B) International division; export department; multinational organization

    (C) Multinational organization; international division; export department

    (D) Multinational organization; export department; international division

    (E) Export department; multinational organization; international division

13. Sugar Bear Fresh Farm Produce is a premium item sold in exclusive stores where freshness and quality are crucial. Which form of transportation should Sugar Bear Fresh Farm Produce utilize in order to get their goods from Colorado to Pennsylvania?

    (A) They shouldn't ship that far.

    (B) Air

    (C) Water

    (D) Train

    (E) Pipeline

14. When a demand curve is "inelastic,"

    (A) total revenues go down if price goes down

    (B) total revenues go down if price goes up

    (C) total revenues stay the same if price goes down

    (D) total revenues stay the same if price goes up

    (E) total revenues go up if price goes up

15. Which of the following is the best choice when large volumes of goods must be stored regularly?

    (A) Private warehouse

    (B) Public warehouse

(C)   Distribution center

(D)   Containerization

(E)   All of the above should be utilized to store goods regularly.

16.   All of the following are criticisms leveled against marketing by critics EXCEPT

(A)   selling shoddy or unsafe products

(B)   forcing consumers to shop online

(C)   using high pressure selling

(D)   using deceptive advertising

(E)   having excessive markups

17.   You finally decided (after some coaxing from your friends) that a good way to get into shape is in-line skating. You **suddenly** become aware of television and radio advertising about Rollerblade products. This is an example of

(A)   selective retention   (D)   selective exposure

(B)   selective perception   (E)   None of the above.

(C)   selective response

18.   Advertising belongs to which aspect of the marketing mix?

(A)   Product   (D)   Promotion

(B)   Price   (E)   Perception

(C)   Place

19.   The way a product is perceived by customers on important attributes is called

(A)   product position   (D)   BCG matrix

(B)   image psychology   (E)   product life cycle

(C)   market segmentation

20.   Choosing a product difference that competitors cannot easily copy would be an example of which of the following kinds of differentiation?

(A) Important

(D) Preemptive

(B) Distinctive

(E) Vertical

(C) Superior

21. Which of the following types of advertising develops primary demand for a product category as opposed to demand for a specific brand?

(A) Institutional

(D) Reminder

(B) Competitive

(E) Pioneering

(C) Product

22. Burdwick's Menswear Store has decided to segment its market based on gender, income, and occupation. Which of the following would most appropriately describe their form of segmentation?

(A) Geographic segmentation

(B) Demographic segmentation

(C) Benefit segmentation

(D) Psychographic segmentation

(E) Behavioral segmentation

23. When a company enters a new product category for which its current brand names are not appropriate, it will likely follow which strategy?

(A) Product extension

(D) New brand

(B) Line extension

(E) Variety seeking

(C) Brand extension

24. Which of the following dimensions of service marketing refers to the notion that the quality of a service depends upon who provides it as well as when, where, and how it is provided?

(A) Intangibility

(D) Homogeneity

(B) Inseparability

(E) Variability

(C) Perishability

25. When choosing the best medium to deliver a firm's message, the first and most important factor to be decided is

    (A) the package design of the product

    (B) to specify the target market and target audience

    (C) to choose the most expensive medium because the most money spent will guarantee the greatest effectiveness

    (D) the products' placement in a store

    (E) the medium the competitive producers are using

26. The stage of the product life cycle characterized by overcapacity, intense competition, and the eventual elimination of weaker competitors is called the

    (A) maturity stage   (D) decline stage

    (B) introduction stage   (E) renewal stage

    (C) growth stage

27. If Mark pays Hershey Foods Corporation for the right to use its name on his line of T-shirts, then Mark is using which strategy?

    (A) Manufacturer's branding   (D) Private branding

    (B) Licensed branding   (E) Line extension

    (C) Co-branding

28. Which type of new product test is most likely to answer the questions: "How does the customer perceive the product?" and "Who would use the product?"

    (A) An internal test

    (B) A concept test

    (C) Commercialization

    (D) Weighted point system

    (E) Non-weighted point system

29. The process of offering a product for sale on a limited basis in a defined geographic area in order to gauge consumer reaction to the actual product is known as

(A) selected controlled markets

(B) store audits

(C) standard markets

(D) test markets

(E) None of the above

30. What is meant by commercialization of a new product?

(A) Create a product prototype.

(B) Test the product and product strategy in the marketplace.

(C) Position and offer the product in the marketplace.

(D) Identify the new product niche.

(E) None of the above

31. Which of the following are NOT examples of support goods?

(A) Services

(B) Supplies

(C) Installations

(D) Accessory equipment

(E) All of the above are examples of support goods.

32. The manufacturing of a telephone, using various raw materials, is an example of what type of utility?

(A) Task   (D) Form

(B) Possession   (E) Place

(C) Time

33. In macro-marketing, which of the following universal functions of marketing have to be performed?

(A) Buying   (D) All of the above

(B) Transporting   (E) None of the above

(C) Marketing information

34. The marketing concept came to the forefront of American business during which of the following eras?

    (A) Simple trade era

    (B) Marketing department era

    (C) Production era

    (D) Sales era

    (E) Marketing company era

35. Which of the following is NOT a step in the approach to segmenting *product-markets*?

    (A) Name the possible product markets.

    (B) List the potential customer needs.

    (C) Estimate the size of the product market segments.

    (D) Form a heterogeneous market.

    (E) All of the above are steps in the process.

36. Which of the following is the best example of product development?

    (A) American Express increased advertising expenditures to encourage customers to use the card when they went out to dinner, not just for shopping.

    (B) To reach new customers, Taco Bell opened new retail outlets in airports, office buildings, zoos, and hospitals.

    (C) Suave boosted sales by introducing a new line of shampoo products.

    (D) Nintendo purchased Cover Girl and expanded into cosmetic products.

    (E) None of the above are good examples of product development.

37. A routine repurchase that may have been made many times before is called

    (A) new-task buying

    (B) straight rebuy

    (C) modified rebuy

    (D) purchase

    (E) None of the above

38. Employers hire buying specialists. These specialists are called what?

    (A) Purchasing agents   (D) Order getters

    (B) Sales managers   (E) Any of the above

    (C) Order takers

39. By evaluating suppliers and how they are working out for a company, buyers can make better (and more informed) decisions. A formal rating of suppliers on all relevant areas of performance is called a(n)

    (A) evaluation   (D) subjective interpretation

    (B) check-list   (E) buyer analysis

    (C) vendor analysis

40. Multiple buying influence means that several people share in making purchase decisions. These people are called

    (A) users   (D) gatekeepers

    (B) buyers   (E) All of the above

    (C) influencers

41. What type of buying is required for nonstandardized products that require careful examination?

    (A) Negotiated contract buying

    (B) Inspection buying

    (C) Sampling buying

    (D) Description buying

    (E) Routinized response buying

42. Which of the following is the first step in undertaking a marketing research project?

    (A) Define the problem.

    (B) Solve the problem.

    (C) Collect problem-specific data.

(D)   Analyze the situation.

(E)   Define a sample.

43.   Which of the following steps of the market research process typically takes over half of the time in completing the research?

(A)   Problem definition

(B)   Situational analysis

(C)   Data collection

(D)   Problem-solving

(E)   Alternative development

44.   A research proposal

(A)   is stated right after the problem is defined

(B)   is a plan that specifies what information will be obtained and
how

(C)   can include information about costs

(D)   Only (A) and (C) are correct.

(E)   Only (B) and (C) are correct.

45.   Which of the following research methods require the most care in
interpreting the results?

(A)   Random sampling

(B)   Mail surveys

(C)   Telephone surveys

(D)   Personal interview surveys

(E)   All of the above

46.   Marketing research

(A)   should be planned by research specialists who understand research techniques better than marketing managers

(B)   consists mainly of survey design and statistical techniques

(C)   is only needed by producers who have long channels of
distribution

(D)   is needed to keep isolated marketing managers in touch with their markets

(E)   should not be an on-going process

47.   Which of the following is a major *disadvantage* associated with the collection of primary data in the course of marketing research?

(A)   It provides the most recent data possible.

(B)   It is typically expensive.

(C)   It allows for secrecy from competitors.

(D)   It fits the firm's marketing needs well.

(E)   Data collection is rapid.

48.   The birthrate in the United States is currently

(A)   starting to drop because more couples are waiting to have children

(B)   rising sharply due to returning soldiers starting new families

(C)   rising sharply due to the abundance of women at the child-bearing age

(D)   dropping because more women are entering the workforce and there is less of a want for large families

(E)   Both (A) and (D) are correct.

49.   The United States

(A)   and England have the highest divorce rate in the world—about 45% of marriages end in divorce

(B)   has the lowest divorce rate in the world—about 12% of marriages end in divorce

(C)   has the highest divorce rate in the world—about 38% of marriages end in divorce

(D)   and England have the lowest divorce rate in the world—about 24% of marriages end in divorce

(E)   has a divorce rate of about 13%

50. A widely available measure of the output of the whole economy and the total market value of goods and services produced in a year in the United States is called

    (A) economic systems

    (B) gross domestic product

    (C) gross sales

    (D) gross margin

    (E) gross national product

51. The income that is left after taxes for a family to make payments on necessities is called

    (A) gross profit

    (B) disposable income

    (C) net profit

    (D) discretionary income

    (E) family income

52. Sales promotion refers to promotion activities that stimulate interest, trial, or purchase by consumers. It would thus include activities other than

    (A) advertising

    (B) publicity

    (C) personal selling

    (D) point-of-purchase materials

    (E) (A), (B), and (C) are correct

53. With regard to Internet marketing, which of the following statements is FALSE?

    (A) Use of e-mail is growing.

    (B) Business-to-business advertising is growing on the Internet.

    (C) Primary users of the Internet are baby boomers.

    (D) Primary users of the Internet are college students and Generation X.

    (E) It allows sellers to learn more about buyers.

54. Managers who are satisfied with their current market share and profit situation sometimes adopt "status quo" objectives. Which of the following phrases would not be used in status quo pricing?

(A) Meet competition.

(B) Stabilize prices.

(C) Avoid competition.

(D) Slightly raise prices.

(E) Promote more aggressively.

55. During the communication process, the same message may be interpreted differently by the various audiences. How the message is translated by the buyer/receiver is called

(A) decoding

(D) source

(B) encoding

(E) receiver

(C) noise

56. The adoption curve, which shows how products are adopted once introduced into the market place, defines several different groups, and how they accept ideas. The largest percentage of adopters fall into which group(s)?

(A) Innovators

(D) Late majority

(B) Early adopters

(E) Laggards or nonadopters

(C) Early and late majority

57. "Pulling" a product through the distribution channel refers to

(A) using normal promotional efforts in order to help sell the whole marketing mix to possible channel members

(B) getting customers to ask intermediaries (or middlemen) for the product

(C) promotion to employees

(D) using only one promotion "blend" for all situations

(E)   using highly expensive and aggressive promotions

58. Selective demand for a company's own brand would most likely occur in which stage of the product life cycle?

(A) Market introduction

(D) Sales decline

(B) Market growth

(E) Competition decline

(C) Market maturity

59. An example of a sales promotion activity aimed at a final consumer or user could be

    (A) banners and streamers   (D) bonuses

    (B) promotional allowances   (E) training materials

    (C) sales contests

60. Trucks are expensive, but much more flexible than other types of transportation modes. Approximately what percentage of consumer products travel from the producer to the final consumer by truck?

    (A) 25%   (D) 66%

    (B) 50%   (E) 75%

    (C) 33%

61. If a firm's total revenue decreases when the price of its product is raised from $50 to $55, the demand for this product between these two prices is

    (A) unitary elastic

    (B) elastic

    (C) inelastic

    (D) static

    (E) Cannot tell from the information given

62. Pure competition occurs when a market has

    (A) many buyers and sellers

    (B) informed buyers and sellers

    (C) homogeneous (similar) products

    (D) easy entry for new sellers

    (E) All of the above are true

63. The firm can vary its marketing mix through the storing function of physical distribution in which of the following ways?

    (A) Adjusting the time the goods are held

    (B) Sharing the storing costs

(C)   Delegating the job to a specialized storing facility

(D)   All of the above

(E)   None of the above

64.   Storing is the marketing function of holding goods. Which economic utility(ies) does it provide?

(A)   Time

(B)   Place

(C)   Possession

(D)   Ownership

(E)   All of the above

65.   The *Wall Street Journal* has been trying to attract new customers by promoting its newspaper for student use in business classes. This is an example of

(A)   product development

(B)   diversification

(C)   market penetration

(D)   market development

(E)   target marketing

66.   When groups of shippers pool their shipments together, what is this called?

(A)   Containerization

(B)   Piggyback service

(C)   Pool car service

(D)   Diversion in transit

(E)   Birdyback service

67.   A tariff is a

(A)   limit on the amount of goods the importing country will accept

(B)   tax levied by a government against imported products

(C)   total ban on imports

(D)   method of entering a foreign market through a licensing arrangement

(E)   boycott of imports by the steel industry of the U.S.

68.   In relation to Maslow's hierarchy of needs, the need for self-esteem, accomplishment, fun, freedom, and relaxation are attributed to which of the following needs?

(A) Physiological

(B) Safety

(C) Self-actualization

(D) Love and belongingness

(E) Esteem, love and belongingness

69. Differences in perceptions affect how consumers gather and interpret information from their environment. The selective processes influencing these perceptions include

(A) selective retention

(B) selective perception

(C) selective exposure

(D) selective response

(E) Only (A), (B), and (C) are correct

70. Countertrade is

(A) illegal in the U.S.

(B) found only in planned economies

(C) a transaction that may not involve an exchange of money

(D) found only in subsistence economies

(E) Both (B) and (D) are true.

71. "Psychographics" is (are)

(A) lifestyle analyses

(B) the study of "who wears the pants in the household" in terms of purchases

(C) an analysis of a person's day-to-day pattern of living expressed as activities, interests, and opinions

(D) an analysis of geographic areas for competitive study

(E) Only (A) and (C) are correct

72. A reference group may influence one's purchases because

    (A) they are members of the same social class

    (B) they are part of middle-class America

    (C) people make comparisons between themselves and others, or try to imitate other's behavior or purchase decisions

    (D) having a mink coat is considered a status symbol

    (E) an opinion leader is a person who influences others in the group

73. Which of the following statements about personal selling is (are) true?

    (A) There should be a desire to combine mass selling and sales promotion with personal selling.

    (B) It has flexibility.

    (C) It is direct spoken communication between buyer and seller.

    (D) It is expensive, especially per contact.

    (E) All of the above.

74. Sending out unsolicited e-mail ads is referred to as

    (A) viral marketing   (D) spamming

    (B) personalized marketing   (E) brand equity

    (C) publicity

75. It is MOST difficult to measure the response rate in

    (A) coupon redemptions   (D) direct mail responses

    (B) billboard advertisements (E) telemarketing

    (C) Internet inquiries

76. Regarding direct marketing programs, which of the following statements is TRUE?

    (A) They bypass wholesalers.

    (B) They target a general audience.

    (C) They are being used less frequently than in the past decade due to changes in technology.

(D) They rely solely on postal mail.

(E) They include newspaper and magazine advertising.

77. A Hispanic fiesta funded by a food company is an example of

(A) sponsorship marketing   (D) event marketing

(B) cause-related marketing   (E) guerrilla marketing

(C) green marketing

78. A local race car driver who displays advertising on his car is involved in

(A) cause-related marketing   (D) event marketing

(B) mobile marketing   (E) green marketing

(C) sponsorship marketing

79. Consider the following scenario. A company's sales force workload is 60,000 calls per year; the average salesperson can make 1,000 calls per year. Using the workload approach, how many salespeople does the company need?

(A) 60   (D) 10

(B) 50   (E) 600

(C) 55

80. During the market introduction phase of the product life cycle, the basic promotional objective is informing. If the product is a really new idea, the promotion needs to develop and build demand. This demand is known as

(A) final demand   (D) tertiary demand

(B) primary demand   (E) selective demand

(C) secondary demand

81. Which of the following is the best response for the statement, "Anyone seeking a profit maximization objective will charge high prices"?

(A) This is always true.

(B) This is not always true.

(C)   Prices will always be higher than the competitor's.

(D)   Prices tend to stay below the competitor's prices.

(E)   None of the above relate to the statement.

82.   A key point regarding sales-oriented objectives is

(A)   a larger market share, if gained at too low a price, may lead to a success with no profits

(B)   aggressive companies often aim to increase market share

(C)   larger sales volume, by itself, does not necessarily lead to higher profits

(D)   it is never easy to measure a firm's market share when determining if there is profit maximization

(E)   All of the above are correct.

83.   The type of price policy that tries to sell the top of the demand curve utilizing a high price, before aiming at more price-sensitive consumers, is called

(A)   skimming pricing   (D)   penetration pricing

(B)   flexible pricing   (E)   odd/even pricing

(C)   one-price policy

84.   Which of the following discounts refer to a list price reduction given to channel members for the specific jobs they are doing for the manufacturer or producer?

(A)   Quantity discounts

(B)   Cash discounts

(C)   Trade discounts

(D)   Cumulative quantity discounts

(E)   Seasonal discounts

85.   Which of the following terms allows a buyer to take a 4 percent discount off the face value of the invoice if the invoice is paid within 20 days, and if not, the full face value of the invoice becomes due in 60 days?

(A) 20/60, net 4   (D) 10/4, net 60

(B) 2/10, net 60   (E) 4/20, net 60

(C) 2/10, net 30

86. Which of the following makes illegal selling the same products to different buyers at different prices?

(A) Wheeler Lea Amendment

(B) Unfair Trade Practice Acts

(C) Robinson-Patman Act

(D) Magnuson-Moss Act

(E) Lanham Act

87. Price fixing falls under which act or amendment?

(A) Robinson-Patman Act

(B) Wheeler Lea Amendment

(C) Sherman Act

(D) Unfair Trade Practice Acts

(E) Lanham Act

88. According to the U.S. Census Bureau, wholesalers are defined as those who sell to

(A) retailers and other merchants

(B) industrial users

(C) institutional users

(D) commercial users

(E) All of the above

89. The most risky and challenging marketing opportunities involve

(A) product development

(B) diversification

(C) market penetration

(D) market development

(E) All of the above are equally risky

90. Which of the following activities do wholesalers perform?

(A) Store inventory

(B) Supply capital

(C) Reduce credit risk

(D) Provide market information

(E) All of the above

91. Marine-Unlimited buys tropical fish from local fish growers. The company takes title to the tropical fish for some period of time before selling to the many pet shops around the area on a cash or credit basis. Marine Unlimited is called a

(A) cash-and-carry wholesaler

(B) rack jobber

(C) producers' cooperative

(D) mail-order wholesaler

(E) merchant wholesaler

92. Service wholesalers provide all the wholesaling functions. Service wholesalers include

(A) general merchandise wholesaler

(B) single-line (general-line) wholesaler

(C) specialty wholesaler

(D) All of the above

(E) None of the above

93. A service wholesaler that carries a wide variety of nonperishable items such as hardware, electrical supplies, furniture, drugs, etc. is called a

(A) single-line wholesaler

(B) general merchandise wholesaler

(C)   specialty wholesaler

(D)   rack jobber

(E)   limited-function wholesaler

94.   Market segmentation

(A)   assumes that most markets can be satisfied by the same marketing mix

(B)   is the same thing as positioning

(C)   tries to identify homogeneous submarkets within a larger market

(D)   means the same thing as marketing mix

(E)   identifies homogeneous and heterogeneous submarkets

95.   Some of the features of cash-and-carry wholesalers include

(A)   catering to retailers too small to be served profitably by service wholesalers

(B)   accepting only cash

(C)   delivering products that they stock in their own trucks

(D)   taking title to the products they sell, but not actually handling stocking or delivering them

(E)   Both (A) and (B)

96.   Sylvia Garcia brings buyers and sellers together. She is called a

(A)   selling agent   (D)   manufacturers' agent

(B)   commission merchant   (E)   rack jobber

(C)   broker

97.   ABC Company segmented its broad product market and decided to target two segments, offering each segment a different marketing mix. Which approach is ABC Company following?

(A)   Differentiated segmentation

(B)   Concentrated segmentation

(C)   Mass marketing

    (D) Green marketing

    (E) Societal marketing

98. The "law of diminishing returns" states that

    (A) the demand for any product will tend to decline over time

    (B) the more of a product a person buys, the less utility that particular product offers him

    (C) if the price of a product is lowered, a smaller quantity will be demanded

    (D) if the price of a product is lowered, quantity demanded stays the same

    (E) if the price of a product is raised, a smaller quantity will be demanded

99. Annie loves her Guess jeans. She wants another pair of Guess jeans, but if there is a brand that has a lower price with similar quality, she will buy that pair instead. This is an example of

    (A) brand recognition   (D) nonrecognition

    (B) brand preference   (E) None of the above

    (C) brand insistence

100. Kenmore appliances (sold by Sears) are an example of a(n)

    (A) dealer brand   (D) individual brand

    (B) manufacturers' brand   (E) family brand

    (C) licensed brand

CLEP PRINCIPLES OF MARKETING
TEST 2

ANSWER KEY

1.	(C)	26.	(A)	51.	(B)	76.	(A)
2.	(C)	27.	(B)	52.	(E)	77.	(D)
3.	(D)	28.	(B)	53.	(C)	78.	(C)
4.	(D)	29.	(D)	54.	(D)	79.	(A)
5.	(D)	30.	(C)	55.	(A)	80.	(B)
6.	(B)	31.	(E)	56.	(C)	81.	(B)
7.	(C)	32.	(D)	57.	(B)	82.	(C)
8.	(E)	33.	(D)	58.	(B)	83.	(A)
9.	(E)	34.	(E)	59.	(A)	84.	(C)
10.	(E)	35.	(D)	60.	(E)	85.	(E)
11.	(E)	36.	(C)	61.	(B)	86.	(C)
12.	(A)	37.	(B)	62.	(E)	87.	(C)
13.	(B)	38.	(A)	63.	(D)	88.	(E)
14.	(A)	39.	(C)	64.	(A)	89.	(B)
15.	(A)	40.	(E)	65.	(D)	90.	(E)
16.	(B)	41.	(B)	66.	(C)	91.	(E)
17.	(D)	42.	(A)	67.	(B)	92.	(D)
18.	(D)	43.	(A)	68.	(E)	93.	(B)
19.	(A)	44.	(E)	69.	(E)	94.	(C)
20.	(D)	45.	(E)	70.	(C)	95.	(E)
21.	(E)	46.	(D)	71.	(E)	96.	(C)
22.	(B)	47.	(B)	72.	(C)	97.	(A)
23.	(D)	48.	(E)	73.	(E)	98.	(E)
24.	(E)	49.	(C)	74.	(D)	99.	(B)
25.	(B)	50.	(B)	75.	(B)	100.	(E)

DETAILED EXPLANATIONS OF ANSWERS

TEST 2

1.　**(C)**　When one wants to calculate the markup of a product, at retail, the correct formula is Amount of Markup = Selling Price – Cost. Thus, (C) is correct. (A), (B), and (D) are incorrect formulas and won't yield the markup. (E) is incorrect because the answer is available from the given data.

2.　**(C)**　When trying to find the markup based upon selling price, the formula to use is Amount of Markup = Selling Price – Cost. In this example, since the selling price is $2,000 and the cost is $800, the answer is $1,200. (A), (B), (D), and (E) are incorrect calculations.

3.　**(D)**　In order to calculate percent of markup to selling price one would use the formula amount of markup/selling price = percent of markup to selling price. Since this comes out to 60%, (D) is correct. (A) is incorrect because $600/1,000 = 60%. (B), (C), and (E) are also incorrect for the same reason.

4.　**(D)**　Their selling price should be $1,000. (A) is incorrect because this gives a 60% markup as a percentage of the $400 cost. (B) cannot be correct because $350 is below cost, thus MOLE would be selling at a loss. (C) is incorrect because in order to calculate selling price, the formula to utilize is SP = COST + MARKUP (SP = C + M). Since the cost of $400 + 60%(SP) is not $750, this choice is wrong. (E) is also incorrect because the cost plus 60% of the selling price does not equal $5,300.

5.　**(D)**　The cost would be $400. (A) is incorrect; the cost will not be equal to or in excess of the selling price. (B) is incorrect; $600 is 60% × $1,000. (C) is incorrect because this is the markup percentage on cost of 60%. (E) is incorrect because Cost = Selling Price – Markup (C = SP – M). Thus, 1,000 – 60%(1,000) = 400, and the cost of the product was $400.

6.　**(B)**　The cost is $400, and the selling price is $500. (A) is incorrect since the selling price and cost can be calculated. (C) is incorrect since

Markup % on Selling Price × Selling Price = Amount of Markup. When calculated, the answer is C = $400 and SP = $500; thus, (D) is also wrong. (E) is incorrect. If the amount of markup is $100, and the markup percent on selling price is $120, this answer cannot possibly be right.

7.   **(C)**   When figuring markup based upon cost, Selling Price = Cost + Markup. Since $200 = $150 + $50, (A), (B), (D), and (E) are all incorrect. Utilizing the formula, $200 − $150 = $50. Remember, this is the markup based upon cost, NOT retail selling price.

8.   **(E)**   Positioning is giving a product a specific image that differentiates it from its competition and this is done to occupy a certain place in consumers' minds in relation to competing brands. The specific positioning tool that depicts consumers' perceptions of brands is called a perceptual map or product space. Hence, (E) is the right answer.

9.   **(E)**   The key to remember is that this calculation is being performed on COST, not retail price. (A), $16.67, is incorrect; this would be the answer if the question had asked for a 40% markup on retail price. (B) cannot be correct because it is at cost. (C) is not correct because Selling Price = Cost + Markup. So SP = $10.00 = .4($10), or $14.00. (D) is also an incorrect answer.

10.   **(E)**   Positioning deals with consumers' perceptions (A). It uses a graphing tool called a perceptual map (B) or a product space diagram (C), and it sometimes incorporates consumers' ideal preferences (D). The only choice that is incorrect is (E) since positioning does not always map brands based on price and quality. The two attributes could be anything that would be relevant to the product category in question. Therefore, the correct answer is (E).

11.   **(E)**   The company must consider each of the elements before entering a foreign market since not doing so could result in embarrassment for the marketer (or worse). Although theme is a correct answer (A), it of itself is not sufficient to support the promotional program. Copy color (B) is important, and the impact of color for the foreign market should be studied; however, it is not the best choice. Product name (C) and the media mix (D) are also important considerations, and are correct, but by themselves they are not the best choice.

12.   **(A)**   The simplest step is to begin shipping out the goods. As the company gets more involved in exporting, they will create an international

division to handle all of the international activities. Finally, they begin thinking of themselves as global marketers, and become a multinational organization. Answers (B), (C), and (D) are incorrect because they do not begin with the simplest step of exporting. Answer (E) is incorrect because creating an international division after becoming a multinational organization is backwards.

13. **(B)** Because of spoilage, Sugar Bear may want to utilize air. In order to increase their market and serve their customers, Sugar Bear may well want to serve the Pennsylvania market, so (A) is incorrect. Water (C) is probably unavailable between Colorado and Pennsylvania, and even if it were, the mode of transportation is probably far too slow for a perishable product. Train (D) may be a viable method of transportation, however, since the produce is a perishable product, the slower forms of transportation like train may not be the best choice for a long journey (unless refrigerated cars are used, and the customer service level is low). Pipelines (E) are not feasible options since fresh produce cannot be sent through this form of transportation.

14. **(A)** Price multiplied by quantity demanded equals total revenues. When a demand curve is inelastic, small changes in price do not cause a change in the quantity demanded. Therefore, if the price goes up, so will total revenues. Similarly, if price goes down, revenues too would decline since quantity demanded remains unchanged. In other words, when the demand is inelastic, both changes in price and revenues move in the same direction (up or down). Only (A) correctly reflects the concept of inelastic demand.

15. **(A)** Private warehousing would be the best choice. If a company stores large volumes of goods on a regular basis, they should probably use company-owned or private warehouses. Public warehouses (B) are best suited to seasonal use. (C) a distribution center's main function is to redistribute the stock, not to store it, so this would be an incorrect choice. Containerization (D) refers to the grouping of individual items into economical shipping quantities, and is incorrect. All of the above should not be utilized given the situation, so (E) is not the best choice.

16. **(B)** Critics often complain that companies intentionally sell substandard products to consumers (A) in order to make excessive profits (E). Others claim that some companies use overly aggressive sales (C) methods to "push" products onto consumers. Finally, some claim that advertising is often guilty of misleading consumers with deceptive advertising

(D). The only choice that does not constitute a valid criticism of marketing is (B) and that is the right answer.

17. **(D)**   This question involves selective processes when one is exposed to stimuli. With selective exposure (D) our minds and eyes seek out and notice information that interests us. In the example, rollerblade products begin to interest you, so you notice ads about them more often. Selective retention (A) occurs when we remember only what we want to remember. This may occur after we have been exposed, suddenly, to the information. Selective perception (B) is when we screen out or modify ideas, messages, and information that conflict with previously learned attitudes and beliefs. Selective response (C) is incorrect because there is not a category called selective response. (E) is incorrect because one of the above, (D), is true.

18. **(D)**   Advertising falls under promotion, which is the communication between the seller and potential buyer to influence attitudes and behavior. Product (A), price (B), and place (C) are all parts of the marketing mix, but advertising does not fit under them. Perception (E) is not one of the "4 Ps" in the marketing mix.

19. **(A)**   Neither the product life cycle (E) nor the BCG Matrix (D) nor market segmentation (C) nor image psychology (B) describe the way a product is perceived by customers on two important attributes. The correct answer is product positioning (A).

20. **(D)**   Preemptive differentiation is defined as the process of choosing a product attribute or difference that competitors would not be able to duplicate. In essence, the firm is taking preemptive action against its competitors; hence, the right answer is (D).

21. **(E)**   Pioneering advertising is usually done early in the product's life cycle and informs potential customers of the product and its benefits, generating primary demand for the category. Institutional advertising (A) promotes a specific organization, not a product. Competitive advertising (B) aims to develop customers' preference for a specific brand. Product advertising (C) aims to sell a product. Reminder advertising (D) aims to keep the product name before the public later in the product's life cycle.

22. **(B)**   Geographic segmentation deals with breaking down a market based on the geographic location of consumers, so (A) is incorrect. Benefit segmentation deals with the different benefits from a product

sought by consumers, so (C) is incorrect. Psychographic segmentation involves consumers' lifestyles (D) and behavioral segmentation divides a market based on usage behavior of consumers (E). Both (D) and (E) do not utilize gender, income, or occupation to segment markets, so they are incorrect choices. However, demographic segmentation (B) does take into consideration consumers' demographics such as income, occupation, and gender. Therefore, the right answer is (B).

23. **(D)** There are four branding strategies, namely line extensions, brand extensions, multibrands, and new brands. These four strategic options are contingent upon two factors: brand name (existing versus new) and product category (existing versus new). Variety seeking (E) and product extension (A) should be ruled out right at the onset since they are irrelevant to branding options. Only in the new brand option (D) does a firm concoct a new brand name for a new product category. Therefore, the correct answer is (D).

24. **(E)** Service marketing is different from product marketing in at least four ways. They are intangibility (A), inseparability (B), perishability (C), and variability (E). Homogeneity is not one of the traits of services, so (D) should be eliminated. The correct answer is (E) because variability refers to the fact that the quality of a service is contingent upon who provided the service, and when, where, and how it was provided.

25. **(B)** Before any medium is chosen, a firm must specify the target market and audience, and know their interests, habits, and behavior. Answers (A) and (D) do not have anything to do with the medium chosen. As many marketers will say, the most expensive medium (C) is not always the best if it does not target the correct audience. (E) is also incorrect, but should be researched after the target market and audience are identified.

26. **(A)** The four stages in the product life cycle (PLC) are introduction, growth, maturity, and decline in that particular order with respect to time. The introduction stage (B) is characterized by low sales and profits when the product is new in the market. This is followed by growth (C) where both sales and profits rapidly increase. Then comes maturity (A) where the product faces intense competition, sales and profits reach their peaks, and weaker competitors drop out of the market. Therefore, (A) is the right answer.

27. **(B)** Licensing a brand means giving another firm the right to a trademark and/or brand name in exchange for a yearly fee (royalty).

Therefore, licensed brand (B) correctly describes Mark's brand sponsorship strategy.

28.　**(B)**　Concept tests usually rely on written descriptions of new products, and may be augmented with sketches of other literature. Several key questions are asked during the concept testing phase of new product development, including "How does the consumer perceive the product," and "who would use the product?". The firm would internally evaluate all new products and proposals to see if they "fit" the product strategy, so an internal test (A) is incorrect. (C) is not correct. A weighted point system (D) can establish criteria for product screening, but does not answer the above questions. Likewise, a non-weighted point system can establish criteria, but it doesn't provide answers to the above questions, thus (E) is incorrect.

29.　**(D)**　Test marketing is performed to see if consumers will actually buy the product. Additionally, changes can be made to the marketing mix variables in a controlled setting. Selected controlled markets are those markets in which the total test is conducted by an outside organization or agency. The tests are conducted by paying retailers for shelf space, guaranteeing distribution to the most popular test market(s), so (A) is incorrect. (B) is not the correct answer. Store audits are conducted by groups (such as A.C. Nielsen), measuring sales in grocery stores and the number of cases ordered by the stores. Standard markets (C) is also incorrect because standard markets are those test sites where companies sell a new product through normal channels, and then monitor the results. (E) is incorrect because there is a correct choice.

30.　**(C)**　The final phase of the new product planning process is known as commercialization. This is when the product is positioned in the marketplace and launched. (A) is incorrect because prototype development occurs in the development phase. The market testing phase (B) of the new product development process involves exposing the actual product to consumers under realistic, yet somewhat controlled, conditions. The new product's niche (D) is defined during the initial strategic phase of the new product development cycle. Finally, (E) is not correct, because there is a correct answer.

31.　**(E)**　Support goods are those goods used to assist in producing other goods and services. Support goods may include services, supplies, installations, and accessory equipment, thus all of the above are correct. (A), (B), (C), and (D) are all examples of support goods, thus each are incorrect choices.

32. **(D)**   Form utility deals with something that is made out of some other material(s), usually called raw materials, thus the manufacturing of a telephone creates form utility. Task utility (A) is incorrect because this is service-related and deals with a person providing a task for someone. (B) is incorrect because possession utility refers to having the right to use or consume a good or service. Time utility is having a product ready for the customer(s) when she or he needs or wants it, so (C) is incorrect. Place utility (E) refers to having a product for a customer where they want it, thus (E) is incorrect.

33. **(D)**   All of the above functions must be performed. The buying function (A) is the purchase of products or services, and is essential in macro-marketing. Likewise, transportation (B) is a required function of macro-marketing, and includes physically moving products to various locations within a channel of distribution. Marketing information (C) is the communication function performed in macro-marketing and is one of the eight universal functions that marketers perform. All three of these answers help make up the eight universal functions of marketing performed in a macro-marketing environment. (E) is incorrect because all are universal macro-marketing functions.

34. **(E)**   The marketing company era saw the development of the marketing concept that states that marketers should strive to satisfy consumer wants and needs, *at a profit!* (A) is incorrect because the marketing concept was not developed or practiced during this era. (B) is incorrect. During the marketing department era, all marketing functions were brought together under one department, but this was not a company-wide practice. (C) is incorrect because during the production era no consideration was given to the market or what customers wanted. (D) is incorrect. During the sales era, a company stresses selling over marketing because of the increase in competition.

35. **(D)**   Forming heterogeneous markets is the opposite of what one wants to do in the development of product-market segments. The marketer, or product manager, should be looking for homogeneous market segments. (A) is incorrect. The marketer should strive to find a name for the possible segments. (B) is also incorrect because the marketer should list the potential customer needs (as well as wants) for each of the segments. (C) is incorrect because the marketer needs to know the approximate size of the market in order to assure profitability. Since (D) is a correct choice, (E) is incorrect.

36. **(C)** Product development deals with offering *new* or *improved* products for current or present markets; thus, (C) is correct. (A) is incorrect because American Express is trying to penetrate the market by attempting to increase current product usage. (B) is not correct because Taco Bell is expanding their market with a current product and are therefore attempting market development. (D) is incorrect because Nintendo is taking a whole new product into an entirely new market or attempting new venture strategies. (E) is not the best choice because there is a correct answer.

37. **(B)** Straight rebuy is a routine purchase of an item that is commonly purchased. (A) is not correct because new task buying occurs when an organization has a new need and the buyer wants a great deal of information about the product prior to purchase. (C) is also incorrect. Modified rebuy is the in-between process of buying where some review is done, although not as much as in a new-task buying situation. Purchase (D) is incorrect because the question relates to a repurchase. (E) is incorrect, because there is a correct answer.

38. **(A)** People who specialize in buying are called purchasing agents. (B) is the manager in the marketing area who is concerned with personal selling. Order takers (C) are salespeople who get orders from, or sell to, the regular or "typical" customer. Order getters (D) are salespeople who specialize in generating new business. Finally, any of the above (E) is incorrect. There is only one most correct choice.

39. **(C)** Vendor analysis is the process used to evaluate suppliers and how they are working out for the company. An evaluation (A) is not the most correct answer. An evaluation is less formal and not as detailed as a vendor analysis. A checklist (B) may be part of a vendor analysis but more information is needed to make an assessment of the vendor than is provided for in a checklist, so this answer is incorrect. Subjective interpretation (D) may be used in analyzing the vendor, but objective measurement is also needed, making this a poor choice. Buyer analysis (E) could be performed by the vendor, but is not needed by the buyer analyzing the vendor. Therefore, this answer is not correct.

40. **(E)** Many people are involved in certain purchase decisions. All of the people listed could have a possible buying influence through the concept of multiple buying influences. Users (A) is a correct choice, however, not the most correct, since all of the individuals listed may have an influence on the final purchase decision. Buyers (B) are those involved in

the purchase process; however, the process may have been initiated by a user or someone else. Thus, even though by itself this would be correct, it is not the best answer. Influencers (C) are those that influence the purchase decision and may share in the purchase decision; however, this is not the most correct answer. Gatekeepers (D) may also be influencers, such as secretaries and other administrative assistants; however, this is not the most correct choice.

41.   **(B)**   Every item should be inspected if nonstandardized products have been ordered. (A) is not correct because negotiated contract buying is agreeing to a contract that allows for changes in the purchase agreement. (C) is also incorrect; sampling buying means looking at only a small part of the potential purchase, and would not be the best method of purchase in this situation. Description buying (D) is the purchase of a product based on a verbal or written description. A routine response buying situation (E) is where the purchaser is making a normal purchase of products purchased before, and should not be used in this situation.

42.   **(A)**   Defining the problem is the first step that should be undertaken. Solving the problem (B) is the final step that should be undertaken, and is thus incorrect. Collecting problem-specific data (C) cannot be undertaken until the problem is defined. Analyzing the situation (D) is the second step, and therefore is incorrect. Defining a sample (E) shouldn't be undertaken until after the situation has been analyzed.

43.   **(A)**   Trying to ascertain what the problem is takes the majority of time in the process. (B) is incorrect. Although situational analysis may be time consuming, it does not take as much time as problem definition, and rarely would it require as much as half of the research time. Data collection (C) is timeconsuming but does not take as much time as problem definition. Problem solving (D) takes place after data collection, and usually doesn't require the time and effort that the other phases do; thus, it is incorrect. The development of alternative solutions (E) again takes time, but the problem definition takes the most time, and in a lot of cases, takes well over half the research time. Therefore, (E) is incorrect.

44.   **(E)**   A research proposal is a plan that specifies what information is needed and how it will be obtained. In addition, most proposals have information as to the cost of the data collection. (A) is incorrect. A research proposal is stated after the situational analysis, not after the problem definition. (B) is a definition of a research proposal and is included in the body of the proposal, but is not the best answer. (C) usually is part of

the research proposal, but is not the best answer. (D) is incorrect because both (A) and (C) are NOT correct.

45. **(E)** All survey results require care in result interpretation. The researcher should be trained in this area. (A), (B), (C), and (D) all require care but are not the best answers for the question. Each must be analyzed carefully and the results accurately stated with care.

46. **(D)** Research is needed to help keep marketing managers in touch with their markets. (A) is incorrect, because research should be planned by both specialists and marketing managers to make sure the user's needs are being met. (B) is incorrect because marketing research is much more than just survey design and statistics. (C) is incorrect. Marketing research is used by everyone involved in the marketing process. (E) is incorrect. Marketing research should be an on-going process.

47. **(B)** Primary data, while costly to acquire, does have a number of big pluses, including the provision of fresh market information (A), providing a level of secrecy from competitors' prying eyes (C), fitting the company's marketing needs snugly (D), and rapid information acquisition. Taken together, the considerable advantages of collecting primary data need to be weighed against the initial high acquisition cost.

48. **(E)** The U.S. birthrate is starting to drop now with more couples waiting longer to have children and more women entering the work force, and there is less of a want for larger families. (A) is true but is not the best choice because (D) is also correct. (B) is incorrect. The only time the birthrate rose sharply due to returning soldiers was during the post-World War II "baby boom," which lasted about 15 years into the early 1960s. (C) is incorrect because the birthrate is simply not rising sharply. This is affected by the fact that there is not an abundance of women at the child-bearing age. (D) is true, but not the best answer because (A) is also correct.

49. **(C)** The United States does have the highest divorce rate in the world—about 38% of the marriages in the U.S. end in divorce. England has nothing to do with divorce rates in the United States. Their divorce rate is lower than the U.S. rate; thus, (A) is incorrect. (B) is incorrect. The U.S. does not have the lowest divorce rate in the world; the opposite is true. (D) is also incorrect. Not only does England not have the lowest

divorce rate, but the percentage given is incorrect. The United States does not have a divorce rate of 13%, it is closer to 38%; thus, (E) is not the most correct choice.

50. **(B)** The economy's gross domestic product (GDP) is a widely available measure of the output of the whole economy and the total market value of goods and services for the United States (produced in a year). The economic system (A) is the way an economy organizes to use scarce resources to produce the goods and services and then distribute them to society for consumption; thus, (A) is incorrect. Gross sales (C) is the total amount charged to all customers during a given time period, and is incorrect. Gross margin (D) refers to businesses and the money they have to cover expenses of selling and other business operations. (E) is incorrect. The term used to be used to define the output of the economy, but was dropped in favor of gross domestic product.

51. **(B)** Disposable income is the income left after paying taxes, which is used to make necessary expenditures such as housing and car payments. (A) refers to business transactions and is the money left over, for a business, to cover the expenses associated with running that business (i.e., sales expenses and operating expenses) and is incorrect. (C) is also incorrect. Net profit is what a company has earned from their operations during a specified time period. Discretionary income (D) is that income left over after taxes and after payments for necessities, so it is incorrect. Family income (E) is money that the family, or household, earns and is incorrect.

52. **(E)** Advertising, publicity, and personal selling are promotion activities and are not a form of sales promotion; thus, sales promotion would not include those activities. Advertising (A) is part of the promotion mix; however, it is not the best choice of those given, and thus is incorrect. (B) is also incorrect; although it is a promotion mix, it is not part of sales promotion. (C) is also incorrect, because it is not the best choice of those given. Point-of-purchase materials (D) would be a form of sales promotion used to stimulate interest, trial, and purchase of products at the point-of-sale; therefore, it is incorrect.

53. **(C)** The primary users of the Internet today are Gen X and college students (D). The use of e-mail is growing (A) and B2B advertising is fast growing on the Internet (B). Internet marketing does allow buyers to learn more about sellers (E). Therefore, all the above statements are true. However, the statement that says that the primary users of the Internet are baby boomers (C) is false, and that is, therefore, the right response to this question.

54. **(D)**   Raising prices in this situation would most likely boost your competitor's position and reduce your customer base. Meeting competition (A) would be likely with a status quo objective and is incorrect. (B) is also incorrect because maintaining stable prices may discourage price competition and leave the situation in the status quo. (C) should not be selected because the manager utilizing a status quo objective does want to avoid price competition. Finally, (E) is incorrect because it's a promotional function that would not be used in a status quo situation.

55. **(A)**   Decoding is the process that the receiver uses to translate the seller's message, and is a correct choice. Encoding (B) is how the seller translates ideas and thoughts about selling the product into words and/or symbols and is an incorrect choice. Noise (C) is incorrect. Noise refers to those distractions in the environment that may create an error in the communication process. (D) refers to the sender, or the seller, of the message and is not a correct choice. Finally, (E) is the potential consumer, not how the message is translated, so it too is incorrect.

56. **(C)**   Both the early and late majority(s) make up approximately 34% (per group) of the adopting public. Innovators (A) make up around $2\frac{1}{2}\%$ of the adopting public, so this is incorrect. Early adopters (B) make up around 12% of the adopting public and is not the most correct answer. The late majority (D), as stated before, makes up about 34% of the adopting public and would be one of two groups who represent the largest adoption percentage; however, this is not the most correct choice. The laggards (E) represent anywhere from 5 to 16% of the adopting public, if they adopt at all. This is an incorrect choice.

57. **(B)**   Pulling is getting the consumers to ask the intermediaries for products, thus forcing these channel members to request the product from the manufacturers. (A) is the process of "pushing" a product through the distribution channel and is incorrect. (C) is a type of internal marketing done to get the employees involved in selling specific products, so it is incorrect. (D) is incorrect. There is not one correct promotion mix for all selling situations. (E) is generally used when the intermediaries do not want to help, or cooperate, with the manufacturers.

58. **(B)**   In this stage, promotion emphasis shifts from trying to create primary demand to that of selective demand. The main objective is to convince consumers that the company's brand is the best choice for purchase. Market introduction (A) would have a promotion emphasis on building primary demand, not selective, and is incorrect. Market maturity

(C) utilizes reminder advertising and promotion about the company's brand, and is not the most correct choice. Sales decline (D) utilizes targeted promotions for specific segments, or targets of the brand, and so is incorrect. Competition decline (E) refers to the fact that the competition is leaving the market, so it is incorrect. Competition decline is not one of the phases of the product life cycle.

59. **(A)** Banners and streamers are examples of sales promotions aimed at the final consumer or end user to stimulate trial of the brand or product. (B) is an example of a sales promotion activity aimed at the intermediary and is not correct. (C) also is aimed toward intermediaries, trying to induce the middlemen to pay special attention to a particular product or brand, thus increasing sales. It is incorrect. Bonuses (D) are an internal sales promotion activity that attempts to motivate the company's own sales force. It is incorrect. (E) is incorrect; training materials are used as an internal method of sales promotion aimed at sales people, so that they pay particular attention to a given product or brand.

60. **(E)** Because of the flexibility of trucks, around 75 percent of all physical products transported by the producer to the end user travel by truck. (A), (B), (C), and (D) are simply incorrect choices, forcing the student to think about how the products they purchase are received and stocked by retailers and other merchants. Although somewhat expensive, products could not reach their final destination if it weren't for trucks.

61. **(B)** In this question, it states that the firm's total revenues decline when price goes up by $5. That means, the quantity demanded must have declined substantially in response to the price increase for total revenues to drop (Price × Quantity Demanded = Total Revenues). This is characteristic of elastic demand curves. Hence, the right answer is (B).

62. **(E)** Some of the assumptions of pure or perfect competition are that there are many buyers and sellers in the market (A), there is perfect information in the market (B), the product being sold is homogeneous among the many sellers (C), and there is little or no entry or exit barriers (D). Since all these assumptions are true, the correct answer is "all of the above" (E).

63. **(D)** Storing is the marketing function of holding goods. Storing provides time utility for the firm and its customers. If consumption does not match production, storing is necessary. The storing of goods allows producers to achieve economies of scale for their products, helping to keep

prices down. (A) is true, but not the correct choice. (B) is also true, but again not the most correct answer. (C) is also true, but not the correct answer. None of the above (E) cannot be true since all of the above are in fact ways to alternate or vary the firm's marketing mix.

64.   **(A)**   Time utility is provided by storing, and is thus the correct choice. Goods must be ready when they are needed, wanted, or demanded by the consumer or else the firm loses sales. Place utility (B) is not achieved. Storage of goods at warehouses does not provide the consumer with a readily available product. Since the consumer does not get the possession of the product through the storage function, possession utility (C) is incorrect, as is ownership utility (D). All of the above are not correct, thus (E) is incorrect.

65.   **(D)**   This question relates to the four types of growth opportunities that firms may pursue. Product development (A) is marketing new products for existing customers. Since the WSJ is trying to attract new customers, (A) is incorrect. Diversification (B) is marketing new products to new markets. Since WSJ hasn't changed its "product," (B) is incorrect. Market penetration (C) is a growth strategy that involves selling existing products in existing markets, so this too is incorrect. Target marketing (E) is incorrect since it is too broad and doesn't specifically address the situation described in the question. The correct answer is market development (D), since it involves selling existing products (WSJ) in new markets (student population).

66.   **(C)**   To offset the shortcomings of low speed and high cost, and still get business from small shippers, railroads allow groups of shippers to pool like goods into a full car. This term is called pool car service. Containerization (A) is incorrect. It refers to the grouping of individual items into economical shipping quantities. Piggyback service (B) refers to the loading of truck trailers onto railroad cars for transportation and is incorrect. Diversion in transit (D) is also incorrect. This refers to the redirection of carloads already in transit. Birdyback service (E) refers to loading trucks or trailers onto airplanes for faster transport to their place of destination. This answer is also incorrect.

67.   **(B)**   A tariff, by definition, is a tax imposed on imports (B). Therefore, that is the correct answer. A quota is a quantitative restriction on the amount of goods that can be imported from a country (A). A boycott is defined as a total ban on imports (C). Franchising is defined as a mode of entering foreign markets through licensing arrangements (D).

Finally, (E) is incorrect because it too discusses a boycott rather than a tariff.

68.   **(E)**   When striving to satisfy basic human needs such as accomplishment, fun, relaxation, and others as stated in the other answers, individuals would find themselves in both the self-esteem needs level and the love and belongingness needs level of the hierarchy. Physiological needs (A) are needs for food, drink, rest, and sex. Safety needs (B) are needs for protection or well-being. Self-actualization (C) is also incorrect. This needs level refers to people who strive for total fulfillment of their maximum capabilities, and is only reached by a small portion of the population. Love and belongingness (D) is a good answer; however, it is not the best choice.

69.   **(E)**   Selective retention, selective perception, and selective exposure all comprise the selective processes. Selective retention (A) means that we remember only what we want to remember, and is true, but is not the most correct response. Selective perception (B) refers to the fact that we screen out ideas, or modify those ideas and messages that conflict with what we have already learned and with our beliefs, and is true, but not the most correct response. Selective exposure (C) means that our eyes and minds seek out and notice only what interests us; we selectively expose ourselves to our environment. However, it is not the most correct answer. Selective response (D) is fictitious. A response, however, is an effort to satisfy a need. This is an incorrect answer.

70.   **(C)**   Countertrade is a form of market exchange in international business that need not involve the use of money. Bartering is the oldest and simplest form of countertrade. Therefore, (C) is the right choice. Countertrade is definitely not an illegal activity in the U.S. (A). It is practiced in planned as well as market-oriented economies, so (B) is false. (D) is false because subsistence economies are by definition self-sufficient so they do not engage in any form of trade. Finally, (E) is false since it claims that both (B) and (D) are true.

71.   **(E)**   Both lifestyle analyses and an analysis of a person's day-to-day living are referred to as psychographics. (A) is a true statement, but is not the best answer. (B) is totally made up and therefore incorrect. This is not a definition of a psychographic. (C) is true, but not the best choice. (D) refers to geographics, or locations of consumers.

72.   **(C)**   A reference group may influence one's purchase behavior because people make comparisons between themselves and others. Refer-

ence groups are the social, economic, or professional groups an individual uses to evaluate their opinions or beliefs. A social class (A) is a group of people who have approximately equal social position as viewed by society. (B) is not relevant to the question at hand and is incorrect. (D) may be a status symbol, but this has no bearing on the question, so it is incorrect. An opinion leader (E) may be part of a reference group, but this refers to an individual rather than a group.

73. **(E)** All of the statements reflect personal selling and are true. Personal selling is part of the promotional mix of marketing. In order to make it more effective, there should be a desire to combine aspects of advertising and sales promotion (A), although this is not the most correct response. Personal selling is the most flexible (B) of all of the promotion variables; however, this is not the most correct response. (C) is true, however, not the most correct response. Personal selling is expensive (D), especially per contact, and that is one of the reasons it should be combined with the other promotional mix variables. This, however, is not the most correct response.

74. **(D)** Spamming (D) is the term given to sending out unsolicited e-mail en masse.

75. **(B)** Measuring the response rate of a promotion campaign is an important aspect of a firm's overall promotion strategy. The task of measurement is relatively easier in the case of direct marketing compared to media advertising. Coupon redemptions (A), Internet inquiries (C), direct-mail responses (D), and telemarketing (E) are various forms of direct marketing. However, billboard ads (B) are not part of a direct marketing campaign. As such, it is difficult to measure the effectiveness of a billboard ad and that is the best response to this question.

76. **(A)** Direct-marketing programs are witnessing robust growth in the current years, so (C) is incorrect. One of the reasons why firms are switching from media advertising to direct marketing is because direct marketing targets a specific audience, thus reducing "waste." That rules out (B). (D) is also false since direct marketing media encompasses a variety of options including e-mail, telemarketing, and postal mail; however, it does not include newspaper and magazine advertising (E). The only true statement is the fact that direct marketing bypasses middlemen such as wholesalers (A).

77. **(D)** A Hispanic fiesta event funded by a food company is an example of event marketing (D). Thus, (D) is the right answer. The only

other choice that may have come close to the right answer is sponsorship marketing (A). However, there is no evidence in the question to indicate that the food company is promoting its name during the fiesta, so (A) ought to be ruled out. Cause-related marketing programs involve a partnership between profit and non-profit organizations to benefit a social cause. Since there is no evidence of a social cause in this question, (B) is incorrect. Green marketing is environmentally friendly marketing practices. There is no indication of this in the question, so (C) is incorrect. Finally, (E) is untrue because there is no evidence of covert guerilla marketing tactics being used in this question.

78.   **(C)**   This is a clear case of sponsorship marketing (C), which happens to be the right answer. In sponsorship marketing, a firm usually pays a celebrity to display the corporate name and/or logo usually on their apparel or automobile in order to give the firm added advertising mileage. In this question, that is what the race car driver (celebrity) is doing on behalf of his/her "sponsor."

79.   **(A)**   A simple arithmetic question. The total sales workload is 60,000 calls per year. One salesperson on average can make 1,000 calls per year. Therefore, in order to find out how many salespeople are needed to cover the entire workload, one will have to divide 60,000 by 1,000. The correct answer is 60 (60,000/1,000).

80.   **(B)**   Primary demand is building demand for an entire product category (i.e., coffee) rather than a specific brand (i.e., Maxwell House). (A) is incorrect because final demand does not exist. Secondary demand (C) is also incorrect for the same reason. Tertiary demand (D) is another fictitious term and is incorrect. Selective demand (E) is creating demand for a specific brand rather than an entire product category, and does not fit as an answer for this particular question.

81.   **(B)**   Pricing to achieve maximization of profits does not always lead to higher prices. Demand and supply may bring high prices if the competition cannot offer a good substitute product. (A) is incorrect. High prices are not always charged in order to develop profit maximization. (C) and (D) are incorrect because the price of competition is usually developed based upon the elasticity of price for a given product or market. (E) is not the correct choice, because one of the other answers is correct.

82.   **(C)**   Larger sales volumes do not necessarily lead to higher profits for a company. (A) and (B) may be objectives but are too vague, and

are incorrect in reference to sales-oriented objectives. (D) is incorrect. It would be a correct answer if it read "...usually easier to measure a firm's market share..." rather than "...never easier...." (E) is incorrect because all of the other answers are not true.

83. **(A)** With the introduction of every new product, there is a group of consumers willing to pay premium prices to try it. This provides an opportunity to launch the product at higher prices before competition forces the prices down. The skimming policy attempts to "skim the cream" off of the top of the market, thus recouping research and development costs early on prior to reducing the price for the rest of the market. Flexible pricing (B) refers to offering different prices to different customers, and is incorrect. One-price policies (C) are policies that offer products to the customers for the same price. Penetration pricing (D) refers to offering the product to the market with an initial low price, and is the opposite of skimming. Odd/even pricing (E) is a form of psychological pricing, setting prices with odd or even endings depending on consumer perception, and is an incorrect response.

84. **(C)** Trade discounts, also known as functional discounts, are given for various activities performed by the channel member for the producer. Quantity discounts (A) are given to encourage volume purchases. Cash discounts (B) are given to encourage buyers to pay their bills early. Cumulative quantity discounts (D) are give to encourage volume purchases like quantity discounts, but allow the purchaser to buy products at different times until they have accumulated enough in purchases to qualify for a volume discount. Seasonal discounts (E) are given to encourage buyers to purchase products early, and out-of-season, to free up space for the manufacturer, among other reasons.

85. **(E)** This billing method is utilized by producers to encourage the early payment of invoices. It helps to increase cash flow for the manufacturer or producer. Most buyers take advantage of these types of terms because it allows a substantial savings on the purchase. (A), (B), (C), and (D) are different terms allowing for different discounts. They may not even make sense, and are thus incorrect choices.

86. **(C)** The Robinson-Patman Act makes it illegal to sell the same products to different buyers at different prices; therefore, (C) is the correct choice. The Wheeler Lea Amendment (A) bans unfair or deceptive acts in commerce. The Unfair Trade Practice Acts (B) puts a lower limit on prices. The Magnuson-Moss Act (D) is a law requiring that producers provide a

clearly written warranty for consumer products. The Lanham Act (E) prohibits a company from misrepresenting another companies' products.

87.   **(C)**   The Sherman Act covers price fixing; therefore, (C) is the correct answer. The Robinson-Patman Act (A) makes it illegal to sell the same products to different buyers at different prices. The Wheeler Lea Amendment (B) bans unfair or deceptive acts in commerce. The Unfair Trade Practice Acts (D) put a lower limit on prices. The Lanham Act (E) prohibits a company from misrepresenting another companies' products.

88.   **(E)**   The U.S. Bureau of the Census defines wholesaling as concerned with activities of those persons or establishments that sell to retailers and other merchants (A), and/or to industrial (B), institutional (C), and commercial (D) users. Therefore, (E) is the correct answer.

89.   **(B)**   Among the four types of growth opportunities described in the question, diversification (B) would be most risky because it involves marketing new products in new markets. In other words, both the product and market are brand new in the case of diversification and that increases the uncertainty level along with risk.

90.   **(E)**   Wholesalers can store inventory (A) to reduce a producer's need to carry large stocks, thus cutting the producer's warehousing expenses; supply capital (B) to reduce a producer's need for working capital by buying the producer's output and carrying it in inventory until it is sold; reduce credit risk (C) by selling to customers the wholesaler knows and taking the loss if these customers do not pay; and provide market information (D) as an informed buyer and seller closer to the market. The wholesaler reduces the producer's need for market research. All of the above (E) is the correct answer.

91.   **(E)**   Merchant wholesalers own (take title to) the products they sell. Cash-and-carry wholesalers (A) operate as service wholesalers, except that the customer must pay cash. Rack jobbers (B) specialize in nonfood products sold through grocery stores and supermarkets, often displayed on wire racks owned by the rack jobber. Producers' cooperatives (C) operate almost as full-service wholesalers with the profits going to the cooperative's customer members. Mail-order wholesalers (D) sell out of a catalog that may be distributed widely to smaller industrial customers or retailers who might not be called on by other middlemen.

92. **(D)**   Service wholesalers can be broken down into general merchandise wholesalers (A), single-line (general-line) wholesalers (B), or specialty wholesalers (C). The correct answer is (D).

93. **(B)**   General merchandise wholesalers originally developed to serve the early retailers such as general stores, which carry a wide variety of nonperishable items. Single-line wholesalers (A) carry a narrower line of merchandise than general merchandise wholesalers. Specialty wholesalers (C) carry an even more narrow range of products and offer more information and services than other types of service wholesalers. Rack jobbers (D) specialize in nonfood products sold through grocery stores and supermarkets, often displayed on wire racks owned by the rack jobber. Limited-function wholesalers (E) provide only limited wholesaling functions.

94. **(C)**   Market segmentation is the process of dividing a large, heterogeneous market comprised of consumers with diverse needs into smaller, homogeneous submarkets (C). The notion of segmentation runs contrary to the assumption that most markets can be satisfied with the same offering (A). Segmentation may precede positioning in the overall scheme of target marketing, but they are clearly not the same thing, so (B) is false. Likewise, segmentation is not the same as a marketing mix since the latter involves the product, place, price, and promotion strategies of a firm, so (D) too is incorrect. (E) is incorrect since market segmentation actually tries to isolate homogeneous submarkets within the total heterogeneous market.

95. **(E)**   Cash-and-carry wholesalers will only accept cash (B). Some retailers, such as small auto repair shops, are too small to be served profitably by a service wholesaler, so the cash-and-carry wholesalers cater to these types of businesses on a cash basis (A). A truck wholesaler delivers products that they stock in their own trucks (C). Drop shippers take title to the products they sell, but do not handle, stock, or deliver them (D).

96. **(C)**   Brokers bring buyers and sellers together; Sylvia Garcia is a broker. Selling agents (A) are responsible for the marketing job for producers. A selling agent may handle the entire output of one or more producers. Commission merchants (B) handle products shipped to them by sellers, complete the sale, and send the money, minus their commission, to each seller. Manufacturers' agents (D) sell similar products for several non-competing producers, for a commission on what is sold. Rack jobbers (E) specialize in nonfood products sold through grocery stores and supermarkets, often displayed on wire racks owned by the rack jobber.

97. **(A)** Differentiated segmentation takes place when a firm offers different marketing mix elements to various segments of customers just as described in this question. Therefore, (A) is the correct answer. Concentrated segmentation (B) occurs when a firm pursues just one segment of consumers with a unique marketing mix. That is not the case in this question. Mass marketing (C) is incorrect since it does not involve any segmentation at all. Green marketing (D) is environmentally friendly marketing that has nothing to do with the question. Similarly, societal marketing (E) is a marketing philosophy that tries to balance consumers' short-term needs with societal welfare. This too is irrelevant with respect to the question, so (E) is incorrect.

98. **(E)** The *law of diminishing returns* states that as the price of a product increases, the quantity demanded of the same product declines (E). As such, the graph of demand versus price is a downward sloping straight line. None of the other choices correctly depicts the law of diminishing returns.

99. **(B)** Annie prefers Guess jeans but may choose another brand if it has a lower price and similar quality. This is called brand preference. In brand recognition (A) you may not intend to purchase the product but you recognize the brand name. If Annie refused to buy any other jeans but Guess jeans, she would show brand insistence (C). Brand nonrecognition (D) is when the final consumers do not recognize a brand. Because (B) is the correct answer, (E) could not be correct.

100. **(E)** Kenmore is a family brand (brand name for several products) of Sears, so (E) is the correct choice. Dealer brands (A) such as Ace Hardware are created by middlemen. Manufacturer brands (B) are created by manufacturers and include brands such as Whirlpool, Ford, and IBM. A licensed brand (C) is a well-known brand that sellers pay to use, such as Walt Disney. An individual brand name (D) separates brand names for each product.

PRACTICE
TEST 3

CLEP PRINCIPLES OF MARKETING
Test 3

(Answer sheets appear in the back of this book.)

TIME: 90 Minutes
100 Questions

DIRECTIONS: Each of the questions or incomplete statements below is followed by five possible answers or completions. Select the best choice in each case and fill in the corresponding oval on the answer sheet.

---

1. Johanna wants to start a new dance studio and needs to calculate the cost and selling price she should charge for lessons. Her accountant told her that the markup percent ON COST should be 15%, and that the amount of markup should be $17.00. What should her cost and selling price be?

    (A) cost = $100; selling price = $90

    (B) cost = $113.33; selling price = $130.33

    (C) cost = $113.33; selling price = $150

    (D) cost = $100; selling price = $19.55

    (E) cost = $13; selling price = $30

2. Freight forwarders can often charge shippers lower rates than basic carriers because they

    (A) will only deliver to selected locations

    (B) only handle large shipments

    (C) combine the small shipments of many shippers into more economical shipping quantities

(D)   do not deal with international shipments

(E)   ship only small quantities

3.   If there is a markup on a retail selling price of $95 where the selling price is $3,400, what is the percent markup on selling price?

(A)   100%   (D)   3.95%

(B)   2.7%   (E)   2.8%

(C)   2.9%

4.   An ad for Chevy's new truck claimed that it is tougher, gives better mileage, and costs less than its leading competitor's truck. The ad specifically named the competing truck. This is an example of what kind of advertising?

(A)   Cooperative   (D)   Institutional

(B)   Direct competitive   (E)   Comparative

(C)   Pioneering

5.   If the regular selling price of a product at Johnson Industries is $500, and the owner, Bit Johnson, decides he wants to mark the product down to $480, what is the dollar amount markdown?

(A) $480

(B) $200

(C) $75

(D) $20

(E)   There is no real markdown because the cost of the product is unknown.

6.   An ad that shows a family seated in a restaurant enjoying a meal after a kids' soccer game and using the advertised product during their meal would be an example of which of the following advertising execution styles?

(A)   Slice of life   (D)   Personality symbol

(B)   Fantasy   (E)   Testimonial evidence

(C)   Mood or imagery

7. Which of the following is an example of sales promotion?

   (A) Price-off coupons distributed to consumers' homes

   (B) A trade show for wholesalers

   (C) A contest to motivate a company's sales force

   (D) Point-of-purchase displays at the checkout counters of a retail store

   (E) All of the above are examples.

8. An invoice states terms of 2/10 net 30, where the invoice amount is $100. What is the cash discount for someone paying the invoice in 25 days?

   (A) $2

   (B) $4

   (C) $6

   (D) $1

   (E) There is no cash discount.

9. The AIDA model in marketing communication refers to four promotion tasks that include

   (A) getting attention, holding interest, creating demand, and obtaining action

   (B) getting attention, holding interest, creating desire, and obtaining action

   (C) becoming aware, holding interest, arousing desire, and obtaining action

   (D) getting attention, holding intrigue, arousing desire, obtaining action

   (E) becoming aware, holding interest, arousing desire, and providing assistance

10. Baby's Notion and Lotion shop requires a minimum markup of 50% at retail on a new line of lotions. If Baby feels that the line of lotions should retail for $20 per lotion, which of the following is the maximum amount she should pay for each lotion she buys?

$$20 = \frac{x}{(100 - 50)/100} \qquad 20 = \left(\frac{x}{100}\right) \cdot 100 \qquad 20 = 1x$$

$$SP = C + m$$
$$20 = x + 50$$
$$x = 10$$

(A) $12   (D) $16.80

(B) $14   (E) None of the above

(C) $15

11. A toy manufacturer needs to store inventory. It would MOST likely use which of the following?

(A) Private warehouses

(B) Public warehouses

(C) Distribution centers

(D) Containerization

(E) They do not need storage; they ship when they manufacture the product.

12. Which of the following would be the *worst* choice when transporting a bulky product, such as coal?

(A) Water

(B) Rail

(C) Air

(D) Truck

(E) All of the above would be equal choices.

13. Pillsbury has one manufacturing plant for each of their products. Which of the following would they utilize in order to get a mixture of their products to individual stores?

(A) Distribution centers   (D) Freight forwarders

(B) Public warehouses   (E) Air distribution

(C) Private warehouses

14. The Horilla Company recently changed its operation to intermesh transporting functions with other marketing functions rather than handling it as an afterthought. By doing this Horilla could focus on minimizing costs for a given level of service. What approach did Horilla Company change to?

(A) Total cost approach   (D) Logistics

(B) Variable cost approach   (E) Quality first concept

(C) Physical distribution concept

15. For which of the following consumer goods would an individual most likely compare price, quality, and/or style?

(A) Convenience goods   (D) Industrial goods

(B) Shopping goods   (E) Unsought goods

(C) Specialty goods

16. When doing positioning, a good marketing manager should

(A) focus on the needs of baby boomers

(B) avoid target marketing strategies

(C) plan on making physical product changes rather than image changes

(D) rely on customers' perceptions of existing and/or proposed brands

(E) focus on what he or she feels are the important features of the product

17. Which of the following stages in the new product development process involves the firm estimating how many units must be sold in order to cover the cost of production?

(A) Idea generation   (D) Test marketing

(B) Screening and evaluation   (E) Development and testing

(C) Business analysis

18. In which of the following situations does a firm face an almost perfectly flat or horizontal demand curve?

(A) Pure competition

(B) Oligopoly

(C) Monopolistic competition

(D) Monopoly

(E) None of the above since demand curves are always downward sloping.

19. The failure of a new product is usually attributable to all of the following EXCEPT

   (A) Too small a target market

   (B) Bad timing

   (C) Poor execution of the marketing mix

   (D) Existence and quality of "protocol"

   (E) All of the above

20. From a consumer's viewpoint, what kind of innovation would an improved electric blanket be?

   (A) Innovation

   (B) Continuous innovation

   (C) Dynamically continuous innovation

   (D) Discontinuous innovation

   (E) None of the above

21. Environmental scanning is an important step in planning a market opportunity analysis. In relation to international marketing, which of the following environments deals with nationalism (putting a country's interests before everything else)?

   (A) Economic   (D) Legal

   (B) Technological   (E) Natural environmental

   (C) Political

22. Which of the following is NOT part of the marketing mix?

   (A) Product   (D) Promotion

   (B) Price   (E) Channels of distribution

   (C) Planning

23. The business philosophy that seeks a balance between satisfying short-run consumer wants and ensuring long-run consumer welfare is referred to as the

   (A) marketing concept

   (B) selling concept

(C) societal marketing concept

(D) product concept

(E) production concept

24. When designing a research study, the researcher must make sure that the research study actually measures what it is supposed to measure. This concept is called

(A) reliability   (D) observation

(B) validity   (E) sampling statistics

(C) communication

25. Which of the following acts were enacted to reduce, or stop, the lessening of competition in the United States?

(A) Pro-competition Act   (D) Clayton Act

(B) Sherman Act   (E) None of the above

(C) Magnuson-Moss Act

26. Reciprocity means

(A) buy from me and I'll buy from you

(B) buy from me or I'll ruin your product's name

(C) buy from me and I'll give you free samples

(D) I'll buy from you no matter who you buy from

(E) None of the above

27. Which of the following conditions are favorable to successful branding?

(A) The dependability and availability of the product are limited.

(B) The demand for the general product class is small.

(C) There are no economies of scale.

(D) The demand is strong enough so that the market price can be high enough to make the branding effort profitable.

(E) All of the above are favorable conditions for successful branding.

28. SIC stands for

    (A) Single industry code

    (B) Several innovative classes

    (C) Standard industrial classification

    (D) Sub-industrial codes

    (E) Standard industry code

29. The United States government market is a large market in and of itself. The U.S. spends billions every year on products and services. Some marketers choose to ignore this market. Why?

    (A) Afraid of not being paid

    (B) Too much competition

    (C) Not enough competition

    (D) Too much red tape (bureaucracy)

    (E) (B) and (C) are correct.

30. Sellers usually approach organizational customers directly. They do this through sales representatives. The use of representatives helps to

    (A) personally pressure a customer to buy from you

    (B) adjust the marketing mix for each individual customer

    (C) size up the customer to decide if you want to call on them again

    (D) see the look in their eyes as you talk about the product

    (E) None of the above

31. Trying to balance the interests of people who want to drink beer and the dangers of losing lives because of drunk driving is an example of

    (A) green marketing   (D) a subsistence economy

    (B) the micro-macro dilemma   (E) relationship marketing

    (C) a marketing exchange

32. The accuracy of quantitative data is affected by

    (A) the response rate   (D) (A), (B) and (C)

    (B) the sample size   (E) None of the above

    (C) the sampling procedure

33. Which of the following is true about a Market Information System (MIS)?

    (A) MIS is a way of continually gathering and analyzing data to provide marketing managers with information they need to make decisions.

    (B) MIS is very expensive and only large firms can develop an effective system.

    (C) The information obtained from the MIS is all the information a manager needs to know for decision-making.

    (D) MIS should only be used when all other avenues for research have been explored.

    (E) MIS should not be used in marketing.

34. The General Agreement on Tariffs and Trade (GATT) was replaced by the

    (A) World Trade Center

    (B) World Health Organization

    (C) International Monetary Fund

    (D) World Trade Organization

    (E) World Bank

35. Income that is left after paying for the family's necessities and which is used for "luxuries" is called

    (A) discretionary income

    (B) disposable income

    (C) net profit

    (D) gross profit

    (E) There is no such definition or word

36. Which of the following factors of income affect spending patterns?

    (A) Geographic location of a customer's family

    (B) Geographic boundaries

    (C) Marital status, age, and the age of the children of a family

    (D) (A) and (C)

    (E) All of the above

37. Which of the following describes the typical buying behavior of the senior citizen?

    (A) They feel affluent and free. They buy basic household goods, and are more interested in recreation, cars, and clothes.

    (B) They feel financially well off. The house may be paid for, thus they may move into an apartment or travel, and they're not interested in new products.

    (C) There is a big drop in income, which means they may keep their home but cut back on most purchases except medical care and other health-related items.

    (D) Their income is still strong but they are likely to sell their home and continue with their current lifestyle.

    (E) None of the above is true.

38. An important family life-cycle category to sell to, and an attractive market for many products and services because of the unusually high income period for the workers in the demographic segment, may be

    (A) empty nesters

    (B) senior citizens

    (C) divorced people

    (D) single/unmarried people

    (E) young marrieds with children

39. Which kind of positioning involves providing the most upscale product or service and charging a premium price to cover the higher costs?

    (A) More for more   (D) The same for less

    (B) More for the same   (E) Less for less

    (C) More for less

40. Why is it often desirable for a marketing manager to combine personal selling with advertising, public relations, direct marketing, and sales promotion?

   (A) To provide immediate feedback

   (B) To provide flexibility

   (C) To save on personal selling expense

   (D) To help salespeople adapt to their environments

   (E) To provide message interpretation

41. Which of the following promotional methods may best be described as mass selling?

   (A) Personal selling and sales promotion

   (B) Advertising and publicity

   (C) Encoding and decoding

   (D) Personal selling and public relations

   (E) Product and promotion

42. The Internet is still having some trouble selling mainstream products. Which of the following challenges would MOST likely account for this fact?

   (A) Skewed user demographics and psychographics

   (B) Clutter

   (C) Security

   (D) Ethical concerns

   (E) Technological inadequacy

43. Sales promotion expenditures are growing and are aimed toward which of the following group(s)?

   (A) Final consumers or users

   (B) Middlemen, or intermediaries

   (C) Employees

   (D) Mature markets

   (E) All of the above

44. Whenever the product involves a physical good, the place variable of the marketing mix requires physical distribution. Another name for physical distribution is

    (A) place utility

    (B) diversion in transit

    (C) logistics

    (D) transportation

    (E) conveyance

45. Transporting is the marketing function of moving goods. Transportation provides which of the following utilities?

    (A) Time utility

    (B) Possession utility

    (C) Place utility

    (D) (A) and (C)

    (E) All of the above utilities are provided by transportation.

46. The total cost approach of physical distribution includes which of the following?

    (A) Evaluating each physical distribution system

    (B) Cost accounting

    (C) Inventory carrying costs

    (D) (A), (B) and (C)

    (E) None of the above

47. Which social class group is matched correctly with their approximate size for those social classes in the United States?

    (A) Upper-class—32%

    (B) Upper-middle class—38%

    (C) Lower-middle class—1.5%

    (D) Upper-lower (or "working") class—12.5%

    (E) Lower-lower class—16%

48. Which of the following is NOT included in the five-step problem-solving process utilized by consumers when purchasing products and services?

    (A) Awareness of a problem

    (B) Information gathering and recall

    (C) Alternative solution evaluation

    (D) Solution selection

    (E) Purchase decision sharing among friends and family

49. A music lover wanting a higher-quality sound from a CD player is most apt to use which of the following levels of problem solving?

    (A) Limited problem solving

    (B) Routinized response behavior

    (C) Extensive problem solving

    (D) Psychological variable problem solving

    (E) Social influences

50. When a consumer experiences cognitive dissonance, this means

    (A) without confirmation, the adopter may buy something else next time he makes a purchase

    (B) the consumer's doubts may lead to tension

    (C) the customer is experiencing uncertainty about the correctness of his purchase decision

    (D) the consumer may seek additional information to confirm his purchase decision

    (E) All of the above may happen

51. Communicating information between the seller and the potential buyer, or others in the channel, to influence attitudes and behavior is known as

    (A) marketing   (D) channels of distribution

    (B) promotion   (E) All of the above

    (C) pricing

52. Which type of allowance is used for new items, slower-moving items, or higher-margin items?

    (A) Trade-in allowance

    (B) Prize-money allowance

    (C) Advertising allowance

    (D) Stocking allowance

    (E) Weekly allowance

53. What is the term used that means the seller pays the cost of loading the products onto some transportation vehicle, then at the point of loading, title passes to the buyer who usually also assumes responsibility for damage en route and pays the freight costs?

    (A) Freight absorption pricing

    (B) Zone pricing

    (C) F.O.B. pricing

    (D) Uniformed delivered pricing

    (E) Loading cost pricing

54. Oligopoly market structures develop when a market has

    (A) numerous sellers

    (B) no buyers

    (C) few sellers

    (D) a monopoly

    (E) a very elastic industry demand

55. Monopolistic competition exists when

    (A) each competitor in the market sells an identical (homogeneous) product

    (B) there is only one firm in the industry

    (C) no substitute products are available for consumers in this market

    (D) each firm in the market has differentiated its product from its competitors

    (E) Both (B) and (C) are true

56. The use of a name, term, symbol, design, or a combination thereof that may or may not be registered is called

    (A) a trademark

    (B) a brand

    (C) a brand name

    (D) a service mark

    (E) brand recognition

57. Which of the following is used by a company to help separate brand names for each of the company's products, when the products are of varying quality or type?

    (A) Licensed brands

    (B) Dealer brands

    (C) Manufacturer brands

    (D) Individual brands

    (E) Licensed-dealer brands

58. Packaging involves

    (A) promotion

    (B) product identification

    (C) protection

    (D) containment

    (E) All of the above

59. "Economies of scale" means that

    (A) the more producers there are in a country, the greater the need for retailers

    (B) larger countries enjoy more economic growth than smaller countries

    (C) as a company produces larger numbers of a particular product, the cost of each product goes up

    (D) as a company produces larger numbers of a particular product, the cost of each product goes down

    (E) smaller companies are more economical

60. Which of the following are important when considering what objectives a firm sets for themselves?

    (A) To engage in specific activities that will perform a socially and economically useful function

    (B) To develop an organization to carry on the business and implement its strategies

(C) To earn the highest possible profits

(D) All of the above are true.

(E) Only (A) and (B) are true.

61. An objective of our MACRO-marketing system should be to

(A) eliminate monopolistic competition

(B) eliminate materialism

(C) satisfy only the very basic requirements of life

(D) eliminate advertising and that will lower prices

(E) continually seek more satisfying solutions to consumer needs

62. A marketing manager must compete for customers with competitors who are offering very similar types of products, and where there are just a few sellers in the industry. This environmental situation would best be described as

(A) an oligopoly   (D) industry leadership

(B) head-on competition   (E) a monopoly

(C) a democracy

63. True work in "green marketing" requires companies to practice the three R's of waste management which are

(A) recycle, recycle, recycle

(B) response, reinforcement, and reward

(C) reducing, reusing, and recycling

(D) recycling, response, and reward

(E) reduce, recycle, and renew

64. Which of the following could be common mistakes a marketing manager might make when introducing a new product?

(A) Incorrectly estimating how long it will take for potential competitors to enter the market

(B) Failing to consider that there will be competition

(C) Discounting how aggressive the competition may be

(D) Ignoring competitors' strengths and weaknesses

(E) All of the above are mistakes that could be made.

65. Which of the following acts deals with deceptive advertising, selling practices, and deceptive pricing?

(A) The Sherman Act

(B) The Clayton Act

(C) The Federal Trade Commission Act

(D) The Magnuson-Moss Act

(E) The Antimerger Act

66. Deciding to target several market segments and design separate offers for each is called

(A) undifferentiated marketing   (D) mass marketing

(B) differentiated marketing   (E) cause marketing

(C) concentrated marketing

67. Which of the following would make up the cultural and social environment that have an effect on consumer's buying behaviors?

(A) Languages people speak

(B) Religious beliefs

(C) Consumer's views on marriage and family

(D) All of the above.

(E) Both (B) and (C)

68. When assessing a market situation utilizing the GE Strategic Planning Grid, which of the following is NOT considered when looking at business strengths?

(A) How long a company has been in business

(B) If the firm has people with the right talents for implementation

(C) Whether the plan is consistent with the firm's profit objectives

(D) Whether the plan is consistent with the firm's image

(E)   Whether the plan could establish a profitable market share given its technical capability, costs, and size

69.   A market-coverage strategy in which a firm decides to ignore market segment differences and go after the whole market with one offer is called

(A)   undifferentiated marketing

(B)   differentiated marketing

(C)   concentrated marketing

(D)   turbomarketing

(E)   cause marketing

70.   When developing a final price for a product, the marketing manager needs to know several things about product cost. Which of the following costs, in relation to accounting costs, is most related to product output?

(A)   Breakeven point   (D)   Total variable cost

(B)   Average cost   (E)   Total fixed cost

(C)   Total cost

71.   Which of the following best describes "value in use" pricing?

(A)   The price the customers expect to pay for many of the products they purchase

(B)   Setting some very low prices in order to get customers into retail stores

(C)   Setting very low prices to attract customers, with the intent to sell more expensive products once the customers are in the store

(D)   Setting prices that will capture some of what the customers will save by substituting the firm's product for one that is currently being used by the customer

(E)   None of the above define "value in use" pricing.

72.   Which of the following is NOT part of a target return strategy when it deals with pricing?

(A) It is a variation of the average-cost method, since the desired target return is added into the total cost.

(B) This approach has the same weaknesses as other average-cost pricing methods.

(C) If the quantity actually sold is less than the quantity used to set the price, then the company does not earn its target return even though the target return seems to be part of the price structure.

(D) Adding a target return to the cost of a product is outdated.

(E) All of the above are part of target return strategies.

73. Which of the following forms of direct marketing has had the most explosive growth in recent years?

(A) Catalog marketing

(B) Direct mail marketing

(C) Telemarketing

(D) Online marketing

(E) B2B marketing

74. A shaver is priced very low. The blades that are sold for the shaver have a higher price and a larger profit margin. The idea is to increase the profits for the blades. What is this type of pricing called?

(A) Prestige pricing

(B) Product-bundle pricing

(C) Complementary product pricing

(D) Full-line pricing

(E) Demand backward pricing

75. Bit Johnson sells four units of his famous BJ733 barbecue grill system, resulting in a total revenue of $420. His total revenue for five units is $460. The price on the four units is $105 per unit and the price for the five units (per unit) is $92. What is the marginal revenue for the fifth unit?

(A) $13

(B) $40

(C) −$40

(D) $52

(E) $26

76. Marianne Johnson Cookies has a total cost for producing macaroon cookies of $102,000. The quantity produced is 90,000 units with a total fixed cost of $30,000. Estimate the average cost.

(A) $3.40

(B) $3.00

(C) $1.13

(D) $1.18

(E) Cannot be estimated from the information given.

77. Which of the following best describes the conditions found in the market maturity stage of the product life cycle?

(A) Consumers view the products in the market as homogenous.

(B) Industry profits begin to rise.

(C) Promotional advertising is unnecessary.

(D) Industry sales are at their lowest point.

(E) New firms can only enter the market during this phase.

78. Which stage of the product life cycle would have the lowest industry profits, where a firm entering may experience profit losses?

(A) Market introduction

(B) Market growth

(C) Market maturity

(D) Sales decline

(E) Sales and profits decline, then rise

79. A "buying center"

(A) is always identified on a firm's organization chart

(B) is always controlled by the purchasing manager

(C) is usually located in big cities

(D) refers to all purchasing managers in an industry

(E) varies from purchase to purchase

80. Which of the following is the best example of the types of firms that seem to be the most heavily invested in database marketing?

    (A) Movie theaters   (D) Automobile companies

    (B) Theme parks   (E) Aircraft manufacturers

    (C) Hotels, banks, and airlines

81. Yahoo!, Excite, and Google are examples of

    (A) Web browsers   (D) chatrooms

    (B) Webcasters   (E) kiosks

    (C) search engines

82. Ninfa is walking down an aisle in a supermarket. Noticing a display of cookies, she suddenly has a craving for them. The cookies are an example of what type of good?

    (A) A staple   (D) A specialty product

    (B) A shopping good   (E) An unsought good

    (C) An impulse good

83. Brian and Frank sell many different varieties of products. All of the products that Brian and Frank offer to their consumers are called

    (A) product assortment

    (B) product line

    (C) individually branded products

    (D) product variety

    (E) product life cycle

84. In a new-task buying situation, a good salesperson should contact the client's

    (A) influencers

    (B) buyers (purchase managers)

    (C) deciders

    (D) gatekeepers

    (E) All of the above

85. Jan Winfield will only buy Levi's jeans. If one store does not have her size, she will go to another store to purchase them. This is an example of which of the following?

   (A) Brand preference

   (B) Brand recognition

   (C) Brand nonrecognition

   (D) Brand insistence

   (E) Brand rejection

86. Good market segments are those that are

   (A) operational

   (B) substantial

   (C) homogeneous within

   (D) All of the above

   (E) international in nature

87. Which of the following sales promotion techniques are generally NOT aimed at middlemen, or intermediaries?

   (A) Trade shows

   (B) Push money

   (C) Aisle displays

   (D) Catalogs

   (E) All of the above are traditionally aimed at middlemen or intermediaries.

88. A write-up in the local paper's "Dining Out" column includes information about your restaurant. This best represents what type of promotion?

   (A) Sales promotion

   (B) Publicity

   (C) Personal selling

   (D) Advertising

   (E) Merchandising

89. In the U.S., transportation rates for goods usually reflect the idea that

   (A) there are economies of scale in transportation

   (B) small quantities can be shipped at a lower cost per pound than large quantities

(C) different modes of transportation do not compete with one another

(D) customers won't pay for faster, more reliable service

(E) customers cannot choose the mode of transportation

90. A selective distribution policy might be used to avoid selling to wholesalers and/or retailers for a number of reasons. Which of the following reason(s) could be given for following a selective strategy?

(A) Retailers/wholesalers have a poor credit rating.

(B) The intermediaries have a reputation for making too many returns or requests for service calls.

(C) The middlemen place orders that are too small to justify making calls or providing service.

(D) The intermediaries are not in a position to do a satisfactory job.

(E) All of the above are good reasons.

91. There are four types of regrouping activities associated with physical distribution management. Of these four, which one involves separating products into grades and/or quality that may be desired by the different target markets?

(A) Assorting   (D) Sorting

(B) Bulk breaking   (E) All of the above are true.

(C) Accumulating

92. Suzanne Marie is a salesperson who utilizes a prepared and memorized presentation of the product she sells every time she goes out on sales calls. This approach to selling is better known as

(A) cold calling

(B) a sales presentation

(C) a canned sales approach

(D) consultative selling

(E) the selling formula approach

93.   Behavioral segmentation dimensions include

(A)   geographic location   (D)   purchase frequency

(B)   age   (E)   social class

(C)   income

94.   A poorly written and worded question that has different meanings to different respondents, when used in a marketing research setting, is said to have poor

(A)   validity   (D)   confidence interval

(B)   accuracy   (E)   sample

(C)   reliability

95.   What type of research seeks to find in-depth, open-ended responses?

(A)   Quantitative   (D)   Experimental

(B)   Marketing   (E)   Qualitative

(C)   Chi square

96.   Tuttie Babe Bikes, a manufacturer of mountain, ten speed, and other bikes, wants to divide its entire market into different groups. One group is for those who exercise, another for those who need transportation, and so on. They want to develop a different marketing mix for each of these groups. This process of dividing consumers into different groups with similar needs is called

(A)   positioning   (D)   combining

(B)   market   (E)   marketing

(C)   segmenting

97.   A segmentation of the toothpaste market would most likely reveal that

(A)   most consumers are concerned about brightness of teeth

(B)   factors such as taste and price are unimportant

(C)   different market segments seek different product benefits

(D)   the entire market can be served with one marketing strategy

(E)   price is the most important selling point

98. The first step in segmenting international markets is to

    (A) develop a marketing mix

    (B) segment by country or region looking at cultural, demo-graphic, and other characteristics

    (C) list the suppliers who serve the market

    (D) consider the list of the suppliers who serve the market

    (E) consider the list of business and organizational buyers

99. The difference between the quantity of products that is economi-cally feasible to create for a manufacturer or producer, and the quan-tity of products desired by the final users of that product is called

    (A) discrepancy of quantity   (D) accumulating

    (B) discrepancy of assortment   (E) advertising

    (C) regrouping

100. Vertical marketing channel-systems, in which the whole channel focuses on the same target market at the end of the channel, could best be described as which of the following?

    (A) A corporate channel system

    (B) An administered channel system

    (C) A contractual channel system

    (D) It could be described by both (A) and (B).

    (E) It could be described by (A), (B), or (C).

CLEP PRINCIPLES OF MARKETING
TEST 3

ANSWER KEY

1.	(B)	26.	(A)	51.	(B)	76.	(C)
2.	(C)	27.	(D)	52.	(B)	77.	(A)
3.	(E)	28.	(C)	53.	(C)	78.	(A)
4.	(E)	29.	(D)	54.	(C)	79.	(E)
5.	(D)	30.	(B)	55.	(D)	80.	(C)
6.	(A)	31.	(B)	56.	(B)	81.	(C)
7.	(E)	32.	(D)	57.	(D)	82.	(C)
8.	(E)	33.	(A)	58.	(E)	83.	(A)
9.	(B)	34.	(D)	59.	(D)	84.	(E)
10.	(E)	35.	(A)	60.	(D)	85.	(D)
11.	(B)	36.	(E)	61.	(E)	86.	(D)
12.	(C)	37.	(C)	62.	(A)	87.	(C)
13.	(A)	38.	(A)	63.	(C)	88.	(B)
14.	(C)	39.	(A)	64.	(E)	89.	(A)
15.	(B)	40.	(C)	65.	(C)	90.	(E)
16.	(D)	41.	(B)	66.	(B)	91.	(D)
17.	(C)	42.	(A)	67.	(D)	92.	(C)
18.	(A)	43.	(E)	68.	(A)	93.	(D)
19.	(D)	44.	(C)	69.	(A)	94.	(A)
20.	(C)	45.	(D)	70.	(D)	95.	(E)
21.	(C)	46.	(D)	71.	(D)	96.	(C)
22.	(C)	47.	(E)	72.	(D)	97.	(C)
23.	(C)	48.	(E)	73.	(D)	98.	(B)
24.	(B)	49.	(C)	74.	(C)	99.	(A)
25.	(D)	50.	(E)	75.	(B)	100.	(E)

DETAILED EXPLANATIONS OF ANSWERS

TEST 3

1.   **(B)**   This is a difficult question. However, the answer can be calculated as C = $113.33, while SP = $130.33. The formula to calculate cost and selling price is as follows: Markup % on Cost × Cost = Amount of Markup. Thus, .15 × Cost = $17. Since $17/.15 = $113.33, this is the cost. Because this is the cost, (A), (C), (D), and (E) cannot be correct. SP = Cost + Markup, so SP = $113.33 + .15($113.33) or SP = $113.33 + $17, which equals = $130.33.

2.   **(C)**   Freight forwarders consolidate small shipments from different shippers and then ship in bulk quantities to take advantage of lower shipping rates. In other words, they specialize in performing the "accumulation" regrouping activity. Therefore, (C) is the right answer.

3.   **(E)**   The markup percent would be 2.8 percent. The markup on retail selling price is calculated by dividing the amount of markup by the selling price; thus, (A), (B), (C), and (D) are incorrect choices. $95/$3,400 = 2.79%, which is rounded to 2.8%.

4.   **(E)**   This question clearly states that Chevy's ad compares its trucks with those of its leading competitor. In addition, Chevy's ad names its competitor in the ad. This is exactly what a comparative advertisement (E) is designed to do. Therefore, (E) is the right answer.

5.   **(D)**   To calculate markdown, the new selling price is subtracted from the original, or regular price. (A), (B), and (C) are incorrect because $500 − $480 = $20. Additionally, a markdown of $480 would make the selling price of the product $20. A markdown of $200 would make the selling price $300, and a markdown of $75 would make the selling price $425. (E) is incorrect because there is a real markdown, and it can be calculated from the information given.

6.   **(A)**   A "slice of life" ad execution style typically depicts an everyday situation into which the advertised product is woven in to complete

the story. In this question, the advertised product is being used during the family's meal after the kids' soccer game. This is a classic execution of the "slice of life" ad appeal. Therefore, (A) is the right answer.

7.   **(E)**   Sales promotions include any temporary incentives directed at channel members, consumers, and/or company salespeople to stimulate a desired response. These short-term incentives include coupons (A), trade shows for wholesalers (B), contests for sales force (C), and point-of-purchase (POP) displays in retail stores (D). Since (E) includes all these options, it is the correct answer.

8.   **(E)**   The term 2/10 net 30 means that if the invoice is paid within ten days, the buyer is afforded a 2% discount. In this case, the invoice was paid after the ten-day period offering the discount; thus, there is no discount. (A) is incorrect, although it would be correct if the buyer were to pay the invoice within the allotted ten-day period. (B), (C), and (D) are incorrect even if the invoice were paid within the ten-day period. The invoice must be paid within the 30-day period as 2/10 net 30 means that there is a 2% discount if paid within ten days, but the net (or balance) due must be paid within 30 days.

9.   **(B)**   The AIDA model in marketing communications refers to four sequential promotion tasks that are attention-interest-desire-action. Therefore, the correct answer is (B)

10.   **(E)**   If Baby is retailing her lotions at $20 per lotion, and needs to achieve a 50% markup at retail, she cannot pay over $10 for each bottle of lotion that she purchases. (A), (B), (C), and (D) have costs that are too high for Baby to achieve her desired markup. Remember that Sales Price = Cost + Markup (SP = C + M). Therefore, $20 (Baby's Retail Price) = C + 50%($20). So, $20 = C + 10, and therefore C = $10. The maximum Baby can pay for each of the bottles of lotion is $10. Of course, less would provide for a greater markup.

11.   **(B)**   Public warehouses are independent storing facilities that are used by companies with a large range of fluctuation between busy seasons (for example, Christmas for the toy manufacturer) and slow seasons. Private warehouses (A) would be inefficient for companies who would only use it a few months out of the year, such as a toy manufacturer. Distribution centers (C) are utilized in redistributing products. They do not specialize in storage. Containerization (D) refers to the regrouping activity of putting items into economical shipping quantities, and is not the correct

answer. (E) is incorrect because the toy manufacturer is more than likely going to need storage facilities.

12.   **(C)**   Air would be the worst choice, and is the correct answer. Because of the high cost of air transportation, heavy items, such as coal, cost too much to ship via this mode of transportation. Water (A) would be a feasible choice for heavy, bulky items if this mode is available. Water would also be the least expensive. Rail (B) and truck (D) would be acceptable ways to transport coal, although rail would be the least expensive of the two, and probably the better choice. All of the above (E) are not acceptable methods of transportation, and this answer is not a good choice.

13.   **(A)**   Pillsbury needs a distribution center to get their desired mix of products to each of their individual customers. A public warehouse (B) or a private warehouse (C) refer only to the ownership of the warehouse (i.e., a private warehouse is owned by the company while a public warehouse has an independent owner), and would not help to redistribute Pillsbury's products. Freight forwarders (D), while they do combine shipments, perform that function for different firms or companies, not for the same company. Air distribution (E), although a potential mode of transportation, is a poor answer because it has nothing to do with product mixture.

14.   **(C)**   The essence of the physical distribution concept is to consider transporting along with all of the other marketing considerations, and strive for the lowest cost for a level of service. While the total cost approach (A) may seem like the correct answer, it refers to picking the best transportation in relation to cost. It does not stress the integration of transporting in the decision-making process. The variable cost approach (B) is not a correct answer. All costs must be looked at when deciding on a transportation mode. Additionally, when integrating all of the functions, this approach would not be considered. Logistics (D) is simply another name for transportation and is incorrect. The quality first concept (E) is a fictitious term and doesn't apply here.

15.   **(B)**   Of the choices given, shopping goods are items that the consumer would take the time to compare price, quality, and/or style when making a decision to purchase. Convenience goods are items that the consumer needs and purchases frequently, but with a minimum of shopping effort; price would not be that important, so (A) is not correct. Specialty goods are items that the consumer would make a special effort to search out and buy, and again, a higher price may not be a deterrent to

purchase. Therefore, (C) is incorrect. Industrial goods are products used in the production of other products for final consumption and are not consumer goods; therefore, (D) is not the best choice. (E) is incorrect because unsought goods are goods that the consumer does not know about or initially want.

16.   **(D)**   Positioning is based on customers' perceptions of the firm's and its competitors' product offerings. Therefore, a good positioning strategy ought to be based on customers' perceptions of brands as stated in (D).

17.   **(C)**   The firm would make a business project for a break-even point in units during the business analysis phase. Idea generation (A) is incorrect. This is the process of developing a useful pool of ideas to turn into products. Screening and evaluation (B) is also incorrect. This involves internal and external evaluations of the new product ideas allowing the elimination of those ideas that don't appear to be profitable or feasible. Test marketing (D) involves exposing the new product to realistic purchase conditions in order to test the marketing mix variables, as well as repurchase rates. Development and testing (E) involves turning an idea into a prototype and testing this prototype for numerous things such as safety and packaging.

18.   **(A)**   When the market faces pure or perfect competition, there are numerous sellers and the product is almost homogeneous. Under these circumstances, individual sellers have minimal impact on the market dynamics including pricing. As such, the market tends to gravitate toward a competitive price that individual sellers have to adopt in order to stay in business. Therefore, (A) is the right answer.

19.   **(D)**   The biggest difference between successful and unsuccessful products is a well-defined target market statement, or "protocol." A protocol identifies customers' needs to be satisfied and includes a statement of wants and preferences. If a protocol exists, chances are that a product will succeed, not fail. Too small of a target market (A) may make a new product fail. Bad timing (B) is also a cause for product failure. Introducing a product too early or too late can mean doom for the product; thus, this answer is incorrect. All of the marketing mix variables must be controlled and executed as planned; poor execution will almost always spell failure for a product, thus (C) is incorrect. Since there is a correct answer, all of the above (E) is incorrect.

20. **(C)** An improved electric blanket would be considered a dynamically continuous innovation. Radically new behavior is not required by the consumer to use an electric blanket, although a slight change in behavior is required. An innovation would simply be a new product or concept on the market, so (A) is incorrect. With continuous innovation, no new behaviors are required so (B) would not be the best choice. Discontinuous innovation involves making the consumer establish entirely new consumption patterns. A significant amount of time must be spent by the seller educating the consumer, so (D) is not correct. Since there is a correct answer, (E) is incorrect.

21. **(C)** The political environment of a country deals with how the people feel about their country and government. They may express their feelings with actions. (A) is incorrect because the economic environment would concentrate more on the GDP, imports, exports, etc. (B) is also incorrect. The technological environment would deal more with how equipped and skilled the country is when dealing with technological advances. The legal environment (D) deals with the country's law and legal/judicial systems. The natural environment (E) would also be incorrect, because the concern here would be the physical environment.

22. **(C)** Planning, although a necessary function of marketing, is not a part of the marketing mix. The development of a successful marketing strategy depends on the effective combination of those elements that make up what is called the marketing mix. These elements include channels of distribution (place); product; price; and integrated marketing communications (promotion). (A) is part of the marketing mix and deals with the development of products including packaging, branding, and labeling. (B) is part of the marketing mix and deals with selecting the best, or most correct, price for a product so that it will be profitable. Promotion (D) is a marketing mix variable that deals with the development of integrated marketing communications. Promotion provides communication via personal selling, advertising, and sales promotion (along with other methods). Channels of distribution (E) is an important marketing mix variable and is the method used to get the product to the final consumer, or end user.

23. **(C)** The marketing concept (A) professes that companies should seek to satisfy consumers' needs with all their resources while satisfying their corporate objectives. It does not explicitly differentiate between consumers' short-term needs and long-run welfare. Thus, (A) is incorrect. The selling concept (B) emphasizes the role of aggressive promotions (selling) that is not compatible with the theme in the question, so (B) is incorrect.

Both (D) and (E) are false because both these philosophies consider production more important than marketing (satisfying consumer needs). The societal marketing concept (C) is the correct answer because it best fits the statement described in the question.

24. **(B)** Validity means that the study actually measures what it purports to measure. Reliability (A) means that the research instrument measures the same thing over and over. Communication (C) deals with a method of gathering data and reporting the findings. Observation (D) is a type of research. Finally, sampling statistics (E) refer to the means used to generalize a sample to a population.

25. **(D)** The Clayton Act's entire focus is to increase competition. (A) is incorrect; there is no such act. The focus of the Sherman Act (B) is to reduce monopolies resulting in restraint of trade. The Magnuson-Moss Act (C) was enacted primarily to deal with unreasonable practices in product warranties. (E) is incorrect because one of the above is true.

26. **(A)** "You scratch my back and I'll scratch yours" is known as reciprocity. (B) is incorrect, and is basically a threat. (C) is incorrect and may be bribery. (D) is not the best answer, and may not be too smart. (E) is incorrect because one of the answers is correct.

27. **(D)** The demand of a product should be strong enough to make the branding effort possible. If there is no dependability and availability of a product (A), favorable branding will not occur. The demand for the general product (B) should be large, not small, for favorable branding conditions. Economies of scale (C) should be present for favorable branding to occur. Because (D) is the correct choice, (E) cannot be correct.

28. **(C)** A standard industrial classification allows potential businesses, and buyers to select, by a code or classification, businesses that may be potential suppliers or customers. Answers (A), (B), (D), and (E) are fictitious definitions.

29. **(D)** Some marketers ignore the government market because they feel that the government red tape is more trouble than the business is worth. (A) is incorrect. The government does pay, although sometimes the payments are a little late in coming. (B) is incorrect; there is a lot of competition, however this is a big market. Not enough competition (C) is incorrect; the government market has plenty of competition. (E) is incorrect because there is a correct choice, and because it would be impossible to have too much and not enough competition.

30.   **(B)**   By utilizing sales representatives, the seller gets more of a chance to adjust the marketing mix variables for each individual customer. Duress is not legal; therefore, (A) is incorrect. (C) is incorrect. You never know who's worth selling to. The least likely customer may turn out to be a large account months later. (D) is incorrect. Although it's good to see the look in the customer's eyes, you still must have the autonomy to adjust the marketing mix, thus increasing your chance of a sale. (E) is an incorrect choice, because marketing mix adjustment is the correct answer.

31.   **(B)**   The micro-macro dilemma (B) takes place when a certain activity may be beneficial for some people but not necessarily for the entire society. The dilemma described in the question describes just that. Drinking beer responsibly and within moderation is fine and many people enjoy that activity. However, the same activity in a different situation may cost people their lives due to drunk-driving fatalities. Therefore, (B) is the right answer.

32.   **(D)**   All of the above are required in order to have accurate, reliable, and valid research results. (A) is required for data accuracy, but is not the best answer and is incorrect. (B) and (C) are also required to give data accuracy, but are not the best choices. Since all of the above are required, none of the above (E) is incorrect.

33.   **(A)**   MIS is a way of continually gathering and analyzing data that can be used for decision-making. (B) is incorrect. With the development of low-cost micro-computers, small as well as large firms can access powerful MIS systems. (C) is not the best choice because marketing managers must use marketing research to supplement data that have become available through MIS. (D) is incorrect. Other avenues of research should be explored, but not at the expense of MIS. Marketers should have an effective MIS implemented for better marketing results; thus, (E) is incorrect.

34.   **(D)**   The World Trade Organization (WTO) replaced the GATT in 1999. Thus, (D) is the right answer.

35.   **(A)**   Discretionary income is what is left over for a family to spend on luxury-type items after taxes and necessities. Disposable income (B) is income used to pay for necessities, after taxes. Net profit (C) is money a company has earned from operations during a specified time period, and is incorrect. Gross profit (D) is the money used to pay for the expenses of running a business. (E) is incorrect because there is a term associated with this definition.

36. **(E)** Geographic locations (A) of a customer's family may effect how often, and when, the customers spend money for specific products; but the answer is not the most correct. Geographic boundaries (B) have a limited effect on where a consumer may shop, but is not the best answer. Marital status, age, and the ages of a family's children (C) affect what type of expenditures a family may make but is not the most correct answer. (D) is incorrect, although (A) and (C) are true.

37. **(C)** The typical senior citizen sees a dramatic drop in his or her income. He or she may keep a home, but all expenditures, except medical and medical-related purchases, are cut back. (A) is incorrect. This would most likely describe a single, unmarried consumer. (B) is incorrect. This definition would most likely fit an empty-nester (older couples with no children living at home, yet the head-of-the-household still in the workforce). (D) is incorrect and would probably best describe a sole survivor who is still working. (E) is incorrect, because one of the above is true.

38. **(A)** The children have left the house, so these people are able to spend their money in other ways. Additionally, they tend to have higher incomes, which can be spent on themselves. Their homes are paid-off, or almost paid off, and their expenses are low. Senior citizens (B) have lower incomes and tend to have additional expenditures on health care. Many divorced individuals (C) actually find themselves in a financial bind, and their expenditures are limited to necessities. Single/unmarrieds (D) will not start off with a high income. Young marrieds with children (E) will find most of their money going to the children and child-related expenditures.

39. **(A)** This question deals with a firm's tradeoff between product quality and price. When firm's provide a high-end upscale product (more) at a premium price (more) they are using a more-for-more positioning platform. Therefore, (A) is the best answer. In contrast, when a firm offers a low-end, basic product at a very low price, it is adopting a less-for-less positioning strategy.

40. **(C)** Although salespeople are included in most marketing mixes, personal selling has the disadvantage of being very expensive per contact. Therefore, it is desirable to include other methods of promotion with personal selling. (A) is incorrect. Personal selling provides the most immediate feedback of all promotional activities. (B) is incorrect. Flexibility is really a benefit of personal selling. (D) is also incorrect. These other promotional activities do not really help the salesperson adapt to any environment. Finally, (E) is incorrect. Personal selling is actually the best way to provide for interpretation of messages.

41. **(B)**   Advertising and publicity are methods of communicating with large numbers of people at the same time and can be referred to as mass selling. (A) is incorrect because personal selling is face-to-face with one person or a small group of people. (C) describes two steps of the communication process, and is incorrect. Personal selling and public relations (D) are incorrect. Public relations, one could argue, may be mass selling; however, as stated above, personal selling is not. Product and promotion (E) are two variables of the marketing mix, and are not promotional methods; thus, the answer is incorrect.

42. **(A)**   Even though tremendous strides have been made in e-commerce in recent years, the single biggest challenge facing e-marketers is the skewed user demographics and lifestyles. Most Internet users are still relatively young, upwardly mobile, educated people. Therefore, the best answer to this question is (A).

43. **(E)**   Sales promotion activities should be aimed at final consumers, intermediaries, employees, and mature markets in order to be effective. Final consumers (A) is true but not the best choice. Firms utilize sales promotions aimed at final consumers to increase demand, or to speed up the time of purchase. (B) is true but not the most correct choice. If the firm wants to stress price-related matters, then sales promotions aimed toward intermediaries may be effective. (C) is true but also not the best choice. Emphasis on getting new customers, introducing new products or selling an entire company line of products would be instances when sales promotions should be used for employees. Finally, (D) is true but not the most correct choice. Mature markets utilize heavy sales promotions when competition for customers and attention from middlemen is required.

44. **(C)**   Logistics is another common term used for physical distribution. Place requires distribution decisions and the correct channel of distribution is critical for product success. Place utility (A) is achieved through physical distribution. However, physical distribution also provides time utility and makes possession or ownership utility possible. Diversion in transit (B) allows redirection of goods already in transit. (D) is not correct. Transportation is just one of the variables, or activities, associated with physical distribution. Conveyance (E) is a synonym for transportation and is incorrect.

45. **(D)**   Transportation provides for both time and place utility. Transportation adds value to a marketing strategy, but adds this value at a cost. If the cost is less than the value added to the product, the transportation mode should be utilized. (A) is true but not the best answer. Time

utility is created by transporting product, but so is place utility. (B) is incorrect. Possession utility is helped by transportation, but transportation alone does not create possession utility. (C) is true but is not the most correct choice. Place utility is provided for by transportation, but, as stated above, transportation also provides time utility. All of the above are not true, so (E) is an incorrect answer.

46. **(D)** In developing total cost for a physical distribution system (PDS), the distribution manager must take into account each PDS, its cost accounting system, and inventory carrying costs. (A) is incorrect by itself because the total cost approach includes more than just PDS evaluation. (B) is also incorrect by itself, but must be taken into account when utilizing the total cost approach. The underlying concept of unit cost directly relates to the cost accounting function. (C) is true but also an incorrect choice. When developing a total cost approach, the physical distribution manager must make sure that carrying costs are not excluded or ignored. None of the above (E) is incorrect.

47. **(E)** The lower-lower class makes up approximately 16% of the American population. The relative size of the other groups is as follows: (A) is incorrect and should be 1.5%; (B) is also incorrect and should be 12.5%; (C) is incorrect and should be 32%; and (D) is also incorrect, and should be 38%. These figures are important for marketers, especially in the product development areas, so they can develop effective products and marketing plans for given markets.

48. **(E)** Purchase decision sharing is not part of the five-step problem-solving process. Although many consumers share decisions, this step should be called purchase evaluation. (A) is part of the problem-solving process and is therefore incorrect. (B) is also not the best answer, although information gathering and/or recall is part of the process. Development of alternative solutions (C) is essential to the process, and is therefore also incorrect. Solution selection (D) is incorrect, although it too is part of the problem-solving process.

49. **(C)** This person is seeking an infrequently purchased, expensive, potentially high-risk product and would most likely utilize extensive problem solving. Limited problem solving (A) would be used by a consumer when they regularly select a particular means of personal needs satisfaction, such as buying a recently issued CD. (B) is incorrect. Routinized response would be used for a low involvement, regularly purchased product such as sugar, salt, or a favorite brand of beer. Psychological variables (D) include motivation, perception, etc., and are not

related to this particular question. Social influences (E) include family, social class, reference groups, etc., and are not relevant to this level of problem solving.

50. **(E)** Without confirmation the adopter may buy something else the next time he makes a purchase (A). Additionally, he may not comment positively about the product to others. Doubts about a purchase lead to tension, which causes cognitive dissonance. This answer is not the best choice, although it is accurate. (B) is also an incorrect choice, although the information is true. Tension *is* caused by purchase doubts. (C) is incorrect, again when, as with the other choices, considered in light of choice (E). When a customer experiences uncertainty about a purchase, this is known as cognitive dissonance. The consumer may seek additional information about the product in order to confirm that the purchase was the correct decision (D); the statement is true, but, even so, does not by itself constitute the best answer.

51. **(B)** The communication of information between buyer and seller to influence an outcome behavior is known as promotion. Marketing (A) provides direction to make sure the right products are produced and delivered to customers. It includes the entire marketing mix of price, place, promotion, and channels of distribution, and is thus incorrect. Pricing (C) is also incorrect and is one of the marketing mix variables that deals with the economic aspect of setting a final price for the product. Channels of distribution (D) are concerned with getting the product to the consumer.

52. **(B)** Prize money, also referred to as PMs or push money allowances, is used to help stimulate sales of products in the above categories. (A) is incorrect, and would probably be utilized with larger type items such as cars or certain types of machinery. Using a trade-in allowance, the seller can reduce the cost of an expensive item without reducing the list cost. (C) is incorrect. Advertising allowances are given to channel members to encourage them to promote the supplier's product locally. (D) is also incorrect. A stocking, or slotting allowance, is given, mostly to retailers, to get them to give the producer or supplier additional, or more ideal, shelf space. A weekly allowance (E) is given to one's children for work they may perform around the house, and is an incorrect choice.

53. **(C)** (A) means absorbing freight costs so that a firm's delivered price meets the nearest competitors, and is incorrect. (B) refers to making an average freight charge to all buyers within specific geographic areas and is incorrect. (D) is also incorrect and refers to making an average freight charge to all buyers. (E) is a nonsense answer and is incorrect.

54. **(C)** A few sellers (C) who tend to dominate the lion's share of the industry sales characterize oligopoly market structures. Thus, (C) is the right answer.

55. **(D)** Monopolistic competition exists when there are many sellers in the market with each trying to differentiate its product or service from those of others. Therefore, (D) is correct.

56. **(B)** Brands include all of the aforementioned, and may or may not be legally registered. A trademark includes only those words, symbols, or marks that are legally registered for use by a company; thus, (A) is incorrect. A brand name (C) is the pronounceable part of the brand. It is a word, letter, or group of words and letters, and is not the most correct choice. A service mark (D) must be legally registered just like a trademark. A service mark provides protection for a service rather than a product, and is not the most correct answer. Brand recognition (E) simply means that the customers recognize or have heard of the brand, and is incorrect.

57. **(D)** Individual branding is used to accomplish the above purpose of separating brands. It is used to help avoid consumer confusion of the products offered for sale by a company or business unit. Licensed brands (A) are well-known brands that resellers generally pay a fee to offer for sale to consumers. Dealer brands (B) are brands that are owned or created by intermediaries. Manufacturer's brands (C) are brands owned and/or created by manufacturers or producers. Finally, licensed-dealer brands (E) is incorrect. These brands would be owned by a dealer and licensed to other dealers.

58. **(E)** Packaging involves product identification, differentiation, utility creation, protection, containment, and promotion; thus, all of the above are correct. (A), (B), (C), and (D) are all true of packaging; however, they would not be the correct choice.

59. **(D)** A firm can exploit "economies of scale" when it reduces its unit costs by operating at high volumes of throughput. (A) and (B) have no bearing on scale economies, so they are both incorrect. (C) is false because the unit costs actually increase when the production levels go up. (E) should be ruled out since "economies of scale" does not refer to the size of the company. The right answer is (D) since in this case unit costs decline as production levels increase.

60. **(D)** When setting objectives, a firm seeks to engage in specific activities that will perform a socially and economically useful function. The firm also seeks to implement effective strategies and to earn a profit.

61. **(E)** Macro-marketing systems throughout the world seek to improve people's standard of living by bridging gaps between supply and demand. The only statement that comes close to the essence of macro-marketing is (E), wherein the role of marketing is described as being to seek better solutions to consumer needs and thereby improve their quality of life.

62. **(A)** According to a traditional economic point of view, most products move toward oligopolistic competition or pure competition as they move through the product life cycle. The situation best describes a situation with relatively few sellers. (B) is not the most correct answer, although it may refer to the situation. The competition may be head-on, or it may not be. (C) is also incorrect. Democracy refers to a governmental environment. (D) is also incorrect. Industry leadership is a descriptive phrase for the company that has top sales, or market share, in a particular industry or field. (E) is incorrect. A monopoly would best be defined as little, or no competition, with one company dominating an industry.

63. **(C)** The three R's of waste management that best embody the essence of "green marketing" are reducing packaging, reusing packaging, and recycling packaging. Therefore, (C) is the right answer.

64. **(E)** All of the answers are common mistakes that could be made by marketing managers when introducing products. (A) is true but not the most correct answer. A marketing manager must count on competition, and must have a strategy that deals with the competition when they enter the market. Likewise, for (B), it is true but not the most correct response. Many companies look to copy successful existing products. (C) is true, but also incorrect. Competitors are quick to respond to good, profit-generating ideas, and will take whatever action is necessary to gain market share. (D) is also not the most correct response. The competition's strengths and weaknesses must be measured. This will allow the marketing manager an edge when competing for consumer business.

65. **(C)** The Federal Trade Commission (FTC) Act is legislation aimed at dealing with unfair methods of competition. The Sherman Act (A) is primarily concerned with restraint of trade and monopoly creation, and is incorrect. The Clayton Act (B) is legislation dealing with policies businesses have that may, or intend to, lessen competition, so it is incor-

rect. The Magnuson-Moss Act (D) is primarily concerned with product warranties. The Antimerger Act (E) seeks to reduce the lessening of competition, and is incorrect.

66. **(B)** Differentiated marketing (segmentation) takes place when a firm offers different marketing mix elements to various segments of customers just as described in this question. Therefore, (B) is the correct answer. Undifferentiated marketing (A) and mass marketing (D) are the same and both are incorrect because they do not involve any segmentation at all. Concentrated marketing (segmentation) (C) occurs when a firm pursues just one segment of consumers with a unique marketing mix. That is not the case in this question. Cause marketing (E) is a joint marketing effort between a profit and nonprofit organization to benefit a social cause. Therefore, (E) is incorrect.

67. **(D)** The language people speak is part of the site-specific culture, and has an effect on how buyers behave (A). Although this answer is true, it is not the most correct. Additionally, religious beliefs (B) held by individuals will influence a consumer's behavior and affect the way consumers respond to promotions and specific products. Although true, this is not the best answer. Views on marriage and the family (C) will affect a consumer's choice of products and will have an impact on selective exposure and retention, but this is not the most correct response. (E) is not correct.

68. **(A)** The General Electric Planning Grid helps managers make three-part judgments (high, medium, or low) about business strengths and industry attractiveness of proposed or existing product market plans. How long a company has been in business is not a primary factor when utilizing the GE Grid to assess business strengths. (B) is a factor. If the company doesn't have the people with talents, such as technical knowledge, marketing skills, etc., the weakness hinders the probability of success for the plan. (C) is a factor. If the product does not fit into the overall profit objectives, then it may not be a good fit for the company. (D) is also a factor utilized in business strength analysis. A firm works hard and spends a lot of time and money developing a particular image. Any product development or introduction assessment utilizing the GE Grid would have to pay heed to the firm's image, and not introduce a product that may conflict with such an image. (E) is also a factor. The firm must consider its abilities and size, as well as the cost of the proposed plan to introduce a product. If a situation arises that is not profitable, or if there are not enough resources and/or capabilities available to the firm to create a positive and profitable market share situation, the market opportunity should not be used.

69. **(A)** Undifferentiated or mass marketing is the correct answer since it defies the basic logic of segmentation in that it assumes a homogeneous market that does not need segmentation.

70. **(D)** Total variable costs are costs such as expenses for parts and wages and are directly related to the output of the product. The break-even point (A) has a relationship with product output, but not directly, and is not the most correct choice. Average costs (B) are calculated by dividing the total cost by the related quantities, and has a relation to product output, but not as directly as variable costs. Total cost (C) includes not only variable costs, but also fixed costs, and is not the best response. Total fixed costs (E) is not the best response because fixed costs have a "fixed" total cost no matter how many of the products are produced. The fixed costs are incurred even when there is no output.

71. **(D)** Value in use pricing refers to setting prices with the intent of substituting a firm's product for one that is currently being used. (A) is not the best choice. The correct word for the description in (A) would be reference pricing. (B) refers to leader pricing, and is an incorrect choice. By offering low prices on some popular items, retailers can get buyers into their stores where they hope, in addition to the lower priced products, the customers will make additional purchases of higher markup products. (C) is called bait pricing, or bait-and-switch pricing, and is incorrect. There are regulations making bait-and-switch pricing illegal in many situations, so the retailer must be careful about what they offer, and how it is offered. (E) is incorrect because the definition of "value in use" pricing is given in answer (D).

72. **(D)** This method has actually become very popular in recent years, and is not outdated. Target return pricing is a variation of the average-cost method since the desired target return is added into the total cost. (A) is incorrect. This approach to pricing has all of the weaknesses as other average-cost pricing methods (B); thus, the answer is incorrect. (C) is a good example of how target return pricing may not work, thus is also not the most correct response. (E) is incorrect because (D) is simply not a correct assumption of target return pricing.

73. **(D)** Online marketing or e-commerce has seen the highest growth rates in recent years among the various forms of direct marketing media. Therefore, the correct answer is (D)

74. **(C)** In complementary product pricing, certain products are priced as a group to ensure sales of a complementary product that may

have a higher markup percentage, and/or that may have higher stock turn-over rates. Prestige pricing (A) is setting a rather high price to suggest high product quality, or status to the buyer, and is incorrect. Product-bundle pricing (B) is setting one price for a specific set of products, and is incorrect. Full-line pricing (D) is incorrect. In full-line pricing, the mar-keter sets the price for an entire, or full, line of products. Demand back-ward pricing (E) is setting an acceptable price for the final consumer (one in which the consumer is willing to pay) and working backward to the producer to see what they can charge. This type of pricing looks to the consumer, or market, to set the price. The answer is incorrect.

75.   **(B)**   Marginal revenue for this problem is calculated by subtracting the $420 total revenue for four units from the $460 total revenue for the five units. This is the formula used to calculate marginal revenue. The price per unit given for this problem is simply not needed and not taken into account when making calculations for marginal revenue. When this calculation is performed, there is a marginal revenue figure of $40 (A), (C), (D), and (E) are not the correct answer, and are miscalculations or guesses.

76.   **(C)**   The average cost is calculated by dividing the total cost of $102,000 by the related quantity produced of 90,000. The most correct response would be $1.13 (although one may have calculated $1.13333333). Depending on rounding, the best, and only, choices would be $1.13 or $1.14. (A), (B), and (D) are incorrect calculations and are incorrect choices. Total fixed costs have already been taken into account with the total cost figure and are not added back into the formula; thus, this figure is not needed. (E) is incorrect because there is plenty of infor-mation given to make the calculations.

77.   **(A)**   The question focuses on the understanding of the product life cycle and its maturity stage. In market maturity, products vary only slightly from that of the competition. Because of this, a lot of product differentiation is minute, and the focus may be on low prices. In addition competitors may have copied marketing variables from the industry leader. (B) is incorrect. Industry profits begin to decline in this phase because of the numbers of competitors who have entered the market. Promotional advertising is necessary during this phase, so that companies can point out their product differences, thus (C) is incorrect. (D) is incor-rect. Industry sales are not at their lowest; conversely, they are at their highest. (E) is also incorrect. A firm can enter the market during any phase of the product life cycle.

78. **(A)** During the market introduction phase, a new idea is being brought to the market. Consumers are not looking for the product, so firms must invest heavily in promotion to begin to secure sales for their products. (B) is incorrect. During growth, profits for the industry actually are rising, and then peak. Maturity (C) is also incorrect. Although the profits decrease during this stage, they are not at their lowest. (D) is also incorrect. In the sales decline stage, profits will eventually become zero; but this is not the lowest of the four stages. In introduction, there may be negative profits. (E) is not one of the four stages of the product life cycle and is incorrect.

79. **(E)** A "buying center" comprises all those individuals who are involved in the purchase decision on behalf of a firm. A "buying center" is something that is mainly applicable to business marketing. "Buying centers" are not identified on a firm's organizational chart; therefore, (A) is incorrect. There is no evidence to support either (B) or (C), so both are incorrect. Since "buying centers" are firm-specific, (D) is incorrect. Finally, "buying centers" vary from purchase to purchase; thus, the correct answer is (E).

80. **(C)** Hotels, banks, and the airlines industry are among the most heavily invested in database and relationship marketing. Thus, the right answer is (C).

81. **(C)** Yahoo!, Excite, Google, Lycos, and others are all examples of Internet search engines. Therefore, the correct answer is (C).

82. **(C)** Ninfa didn't plan on buying the cookies, but when she saw them she had a craving to eat those cookies. The cookies were an unplanned purchase, but were purchased because of a strong sudden need; thus, the cookies are impulse goods. (A) is incorrect because a staple good is one that is purchased often and without much thought. Milk and bread are good examples of staples. Shopping goods (B) are products that are sought after. They take time and energy to find, but are worth that effort; thus, shopping goods is not the most correct response. (D) is incorrect. Specialty goods are products that the person will spend a large amount of time seeking out. Additionally, a lot of effort goes into finding and purchasing specialty goods. (E) is also incorrect. An unsought good is a product that a customer would not want, or perhaps doesn't even know about. Ninfa had seen or heard about the cookies, so they are not unsought goods.

83.   **(A)**   A product assortment is all of the individual products offered for sale to consumers. (B) is incorrect, because a product line is a set of individual products that are closely related by type of product, style, price, or some other characteristic. For example, if Brian and Frank sold shampoos, then all of their shampoo offerings would be a product line. (C) is incorrect. The individually branded product is a single product, not a group of products. A single bottle of Frank's Brand shampoo may be an example of an individually branded product. (D) is incorrect because product variety is not a marketing term. It may be a term in consumer language that would refer to a retailer's mix of products. (E) is incorrect. A product life cycle is a concept used to measure where a product is in reference to an entire industry.

84.   **(E)**   A new-task buying situation is one in which a firm typically faces a new problem that requires the collective wisdom of several key decision makers within an organization. It is therefore recommended that a salesperson contact each one of the decision makers who are involved in the buying decision including the influencers (A), buyers (B), deciders (C), and gatekeepers (D). Since (E) includes all of these options, it is the best answer for this question.

85.   **(D)**   Jan will buy only Levi's jeans, and refuses to substitute another product for them. She is willing to shop around until she finds the Levi's that fit. Brand preference (A) is incorrect. Jan doesn't prefer Levi's, she will only buy Levi's. With brand preference, Jan would buy Levi's over a competing brand, however would be willing to settle for another brand if Levi's weren't available. (B) is incorrect. Brand recognition refers to the fact that the customer remembers, or recognizes, the brand or brand name. This doesn't include always buying, or even usually buying, the product. In fact, with brand recognition the consumer may have never tried the product or brand. (C) refers to the consumer not recognizing the brand, and is incorrect. If the customer doesn't remember the brand, they are not going to insist on purchasing it. Brand rejection (E) is incorrect. With brand rejection, the consumer will not purchase a particular brand for some reason, which usually deals with the brand's image.

86.   **(D)**   This question relates to the criteria for good segmentation. Among other things, good segments need to be easily accessible and operational (A), they should be substantial enough to be profitable (B), and people within the same segment should be similar in their responses to marketing stimuli—homogeneous within (C). Good segments do not necessarily have to be international in nature. Therefore, (E) should be ruled out. The correct answer is (D) since it claims that (A), (B), and (C) are true.

87. **(C)** Aisle displays are generally aimed at the final consumer or user of the good, and are frequently seen in retail stores, especially grocery stores. Trade shows (A) are aimed toward the intermediaries and try to solicit orders for particular types of products. Push money (B) is given to intermediaries in order to encourage them to pay particular attention to a manufacturer's product or product line. This is an incorrect response. Catalogs (D) are sent to intermediaries to give additional product information, such as discounts, price, technical data, etc.; this is an incorrect answer. Final consumers may also utilize catalogs. (E) is incorrect, because all of the above are not traditional methods of promoting to intermediaries or middlemen.

88. **(B)** Publicity is an unpaid form of nonpersonal communication. Sales promotion (A) refers to those activities that support advertising and personal selling. Point-of-purchase displays, contests, and sweepstakes would be examples of sales promotion; however, a write-up in a local column is not a type of sales promotion. Thus, this response is incorrect. (C) is incorrect. Personal selling is one-on-one (or a few-on-a-few), direct, personal communication. It doesn't use mass media, but is personal. Advertising (D) is paid communication that deals with a "mass" audience. Publicity is unpaid, and thus advertising is incorrect. Merchandising (E) is either in-store, or used to sell intermediaries. It generally does not utilize a mass media, and it is paid for. Thus, the answer is not the most correct.

89. **(A)** Transportation rates are usually lower for bulk shipments compared to partial carload cargo. This means that shippers can experience "economies of scale" if they ship goods in bulk (A). Therefore, the correct answer is (A). Small quantities cost more to ship than larger quantities, so (B) is false. The different modes of cargo transportation, i.e., trucks, rail, ships, and airplanes often compete with one another, so (C) is untrue. (D) is also false since customers are sometimes willing to pay higher rates for faster and more reliable service. Finally, (E) is false since customers can often choose the mode of transportation.

90. **(E)** The question deals with the establishment of a selective distribution policy that is used to avoid sales to certain intermediaries. All of the reasons stated are excellent reasons to utilize this type of distribution. (A) is true but not the most correct response. Poor credit translates to inefficient use of cash for the producer or manufacturer, and perhaps a poor cash flow. Too many returns (B) cause additional expenses for the

producer in terms of human and capital resources. If there is only one intermediary making these returns, the problem is probably with the channel member and not the products themselves. In order to create economies of scale, the producers need to produce in large enough amounts to make cost of the product competitive with other products on the market. Sales in very small amounts cost the manufacturer (C). If there are numerous small accounts, the manufacturer may want to consider utilizing distributors for their products. Thus (C) is true, but not the most correct response. (D) is also true, but not the most correct response. If the intermediary channel member cannot help with product sales in a satisfactory (or better) manner, than the manufacturer may want to avoid doing business with them.

91. **(D)** There are four types of regrouping activities: assorting, bulk breaking, accumulating, and sorting. Sorting involves placing products into special categories by quality and/or grades, to help satisfy the targeted markets. Assorting (A) involves putting together a variety of products to give the target market(s) the assortment they want and need. Bulk breaking (B) involves the division of larger quantities into smaller ones during the channel of distribution. As the product gets closer and closer to the final user, more bulk breaking occurs. This answer is incorrect. Accumulating (C) involves collecting products from many small manufacturers or producers so that a shipment of these products can be offered or sold to other members of the channel. (E) is incorrect because sorting is the name of the process used to separate products based upon grade or quality (or both) for the targeted markets.

92. **(C)** Any prepared sales presentation where the salesperson doesn't vary from the "script" is called a canned, or prepared, approach. Cold calling (A) is the process of calling on customers without an appointment. They may or may not have a need for the product. The prospective buyer does not contact the company (or create a "lead") in cold calling. A sales presentation (B) would include all of the approaches taken in selling. Quite simply, a sales presentation is an attempt at making a sale. Consultative selling (D) is when the potential customer is asked (or consulted) about their needs and wants in a product. The presentation is modified each time a call is made depending on the potential customer's needs. A close is not attempted in consultative selling until the customer's needs are determined. The selling formula approach (E) is not the most correct response. In sales formula selling, the salesperson begins with a prepared presentation, or outline, and then takes the potential buyer through a series of logical steps (based upon the outline) in an attempt to close the sale.

93. **(D)** Behavioral segmentation deals with consumers' usage be-havior, such as usage rate, usage occasion, or purchase frequency (D). Therefore, (D) is the right choice for this question. Geographic location (A) is a geographic segmentation variable. Age (B) and income (C) are demographic segmentation variables. Finally, social class (E) is a psycho-graphic segmentation variable.

94. **(A)** Validity is the extent that a research instrument (such as a questionnaire) measures what it purports, or is intended, to measure. If the question has a different meaning to different people, it is invalid. (B) is incorrect. Accuracy refers to the extent that collected data are error free. A poorly worded question may not have an impact on accuracy. Reliability (C) is incorrect. Reliability refers to the fact that the questionnaire, or research instrument, measures the same thing over and over. Thus, every time the instrument is used it measures the same thing. The research can be reliable; however, it still may not be valid. In other words it is measur-ing the incorrect thing over and over. (D) is incorrect. Confidence inter-vals have to do with sampling accuracy. A confidence interval is the range on either side of an estimate that would likely contain the true population values. Samples (E) have nothing to do with question wording, and is thus incorrect. Samples are small portions of a population under study that should reflect the overall population.

95. **(E)** By definition, qualitative research seeks to find in-depth, open-ended responses to questions posed. This type of research tries to elicit thoughts respondents may have about a particular topic without giv-ing too many guidelines. Quantitative research (A) seeks structured re-sponses that can be summarized and generalized to populations; thus, this response is incorrect. Marketing research (B) includes both quantitative and qualitative data, and is too broad a category. Chi square (C) is also incorrect. This is a statistical technique used to help summarize quantita-tive data. Experimental (D) is also incorrect. In an experimental setting the researcher would generally use quantitative data.

96. **(C)** This is the process of clustering people, current or potential consumers, into groups or segments with like needs or wants. (A) is incor-rect. Positioning defines how consumers view brands in a market. (B) is not the most correct response. A market refers to the entire population who may have a need for a product. No thought is given to breaking the market down into smaller homogenous groups or segments. (D) is also incorrect. Combiners take the smaller segments and combine them into larger subgroups. And finally, marketing (E) is the entire process of get-

ting a product or service from the producer to the final consumer, and thus is not the best response.

97. **(C)** If one were to segment the toothpaste market, it would be logical to assume that different consumer segments would seek different product benefits (C). For instance, kids may want a good-tasting, sparkly toothpaste, while socializers may want breath-freshening toothpaste and so on. Therefore, (C) is the correct answer. The other choices can be ruled out since there is no logical basis to make such assumptions.

98. **(B)** In international segmentation, the first step usually involves a broad, macro-level decision based on the target countries' demographic, cultural, and political environments. If the macro-environment looks favorable, then the firm proceeds with a more detailed, micro-analysis of the market characteristics. As such, (B) is the correct answer.

99. **(A)** A producer wishes to take advantage of economies of scale when producing a product. In other words as the number produced increases, the cost per unit (not total costs) goes down. Thus, it is economically advantageous to produce in greater numbers. Consumers don't want to consume in large numbers; they have a need for smaller amounts of product for consumption. This difference is referred to as a discrepancy of quantity. (B) is incorrect. Discrepancy of assortment is the difference in the types of products produced by a manufacturer and needed or wanted, by consumers. Regrouping (C) refers to adjusting the quantities and/or assortments of products handled at each level of the channel of distribution, so it is incorrect. Accumulating (D) involves the collection of products from smaller producers, thus is incorrect. Advertising (E) involves communicating, in a nonpersonal atmosphere, via some type of medium, with large numbers of consumers or potential consumers.

100. **(E)** Vertical marketing channels of distribution can be a corporate channel (A) where the corporation owns the entire channel of distribution. However, this is not the best response. It can be an administered channel (B) where the channel members informally agree on which services the channel members will perform; however, this is not the most correct response. A vertical channel system could also be contractual (C) where the members agree, by contract, to cooperate with each other, and also which functions should be provided by each of the members. This, however, is not the most correct response. (D) is true, both corporate channels and administered channels could provide or develop a vertical channel system, however, so could a system under contract, which (D) leaves out. Thus, this is not the best response.

ANSWER SHEETS

ADDITIONAL
ANSWER
SHEETS

CLEP PRINCIPLES OF MARKETING – TEST __

1. Ⓐ Ⓑ Ⓒ Ⓓ Ⓔ	35. Ⓐ Ⓑ Ⓒ Ⓓ Ⓔ	69. Ⓐ Ⓑ Ⓒ Ⓓ Ⓔ
2. Ⓐ Ⓑ Ⓒ Ⓓ Ⓔ	36. Ⓐ Ⓑ Ⓒ Ⓓ Ⓔ	70. Ⓐ Ⓑ Ⓒ Ⓓ Ⓔ
3. Ⓐ Ⓑ Ⓒ Ⓓ Ⓔ	37. Ⓐ Ⓑ Ⓒ Ⓓ Ⓔ	71. Ⓐ Ⓑ Ⓒ Ⓓ Ⓔ
4. Ⓐ Ⓑ Ⓒ Ⓓ Ⓔ	38. Ⓐ Ⓑ Ⓒ Ⓓ Ⓔ	72. Ⓐ Ⓑ Ⓒ Ⓓ Ⓔ
5. Ⓐ Ⓑ Ⓒ Ⓓ Ⓔ	39. Ⓐ Ⓑ Ⓒ Ⓓ Ⓔ	73. Ⓐ Ⓑ Ⓒ Ⓓ Ⓔ
6. Ⓐ Ⓑ Ⓒ Ⓓ Ⓔ	40. Ⓐ Ⓑ Ⓒ Ⓓ Ⓔ	74. Ⓐ Ⓑ Ⓒ Ⓓ Ⓔ
7. Ⓐ Ⓑ Ⓒ Ⓓ Ⓔ	41. Ⓐ Ⓑ Ⓒ Ⓓ Ⓔ	75. Ⓐ Ⓑ Ⓒ Ⓓ Ⓔ
8. Ⓐ Ⓑ Ⓒ Ⓓ Ⓔ	42. Ⓐ Ⓑ Ⓒ Ⓓ Ⓔ	76. Ⓐ Ⓑ Ⓒ Ⓓ Ⓔ
9. Ⓐ Ⓑ Ⓒ Ⓓ Ⓔ	43. Ⓐ Ⓑ Ⓒ Ⓓ Ⓔ	77. Ⓐ Ⓑ Ⓒ Ⓓ Ⓔ
10. Ⓐ Ⓑ Ⓒ Ⓓ Ⓔ	44. Ⓐ Ⓑ Ⓒ Ⓓ Ⓔ	78. Ⓐ Ⓑ Ⓒ Ⓓ Ⓔ
11. Ⓐ Ⓑ Ⓒ Ⓓ Ⓔ	45. Ⓐ Ⓑ Ⓒ Ⓓ Ⓔ	79. Ⓐ Ⓑ Ⓒ Ⓓ Ⓔ
12. Ⓐ Ⓑ Ⓒ Ⓓ Ⓔ	46. Ⓐ Ⓑ Ⓒ Ⓓ Ⓔ	80. Ⓐ Ⓑ Ⓒ Ⓓ Ⓔ
13. Ⓐ Ⓑ Ⓒ Ⓓ Ⓔ	47. Ⓐ Ⓑ Ⓒ Ⓓ Ⓔ	81. Ⓐ Ⓑ Ⓒ Ⓓ Ⓔ
14. Ⓐ Ⓑ Ⓒ Ⓓ Ⓔ	48. Ⓐ Ⓑ Ⓒ Ⓓ Ⓔ	82. Ⓐ Ⓑ Ⓒ Ⓓ Ⓔ
15. Ⓐ Ⓑ Ⓒ Ⓓ Ⓔ	49. Ⓐ Ⓑ Ⓒ Ⓓ Ⓔ	83. Ⓐ Ⓑ Ⓒ Ⓓ Ⓔ
16. Ⓐ Ⓑ Ⓒ Ⓓ Ⓔ	50. Ⓐ Ⓑ Ⓒ Ⓓ Ⓔ	84. Ⓐ Ⓑ Ⓒ Ⓓ Ⓔ
17. Ⓐ Ⓑ Ⓒ Ⓓ Ⓔ	51. Ⓐ Ⓑ Ⓒ Ⓓ Ⓔ	85. Ⓐ Ⓑ Ⓒ Ⓓ Ⓔ
18. Ⓐ Ⓑ Ⓒ Ⓓ Ⓔ	52. Ⓐ Ⓑ Ⓒ Ⓓ Ⓔ	86. Ⓐ Ⓑ Ⓒ Ⓓ Ⓔ
19. Ⓐ Ⓑ Ⓒ Ⓓ Ⓔ	53. Ⓐ Ⓑ Ⓒ Ⓓ Ⓔ	87. Ⓐ Ⓑ Ⓒ Ⓓ Ⓔ
20. Ⓐ Ⓑ Ⓒ Ⓓ Ⓔ	54. Ⓐ Ⓑ Ⓒ Ⓓ Ⓔ	88. Ⓐ Ⓑ Ⓒ Ⓓ Ⓔ
21. Ⓐ Ⓑ Ⓒ Ⓓ Ⓔ	55. Ⓐ Ⓑ Ⓒ Ⓓ Ⓔ	89. Ⓐ Ⓑ Ⓒ Ⓓ Ⓔ
22. Ⓐ Ⓑ Ⓒ Ⓓ Ⓔ	56. Ⓐ Ⓑ Ⓒ Ⓓ Ⓔ	90. Ⓐ Ⓑ Ⓒ Ⓓ Ⓔ
23. Ⓐ Ⓑ Ⓒ Ⓓ Ⓔ	57. Ⓐ Ⓑ Ⓒ Ⓓ Ⓔ	91. Ⓐ Ⓑ Ⓒ Ⓓ Ⓔ
24. Ⓐ Ⓑ Ⓒ Ⓓ Ⓔ	58. Ⓐ Ⓑ Ⓒ Ⓓ Ⓔ	92. Ⓐ Ⓑ Ⓒ Ⓓ Ⓔ
25. Ⓐ Ⓑ Ⓒ Ⓓ Ⓔ	59. Ⓐ Ⓑ Ⓒ Ⓓ Ⓔ	93. Ⓐ Ⓑ Ⓒ Ⓓ Ⓔ
26. Ⓐ Ⓑ Ⓒ Ⓓ Ⓔ	60. Ⓐ Ⓑ Ⓒ Ⓓ Ⓔ	94. Ⓐ Ⓑ Ⓒ Ⓓ Ⓔ
27. Ⓐ Ⓑ Ⓒ Ⓓ Ⓔ	61. Ⓐ Ⓑ Ⓒ Ⓓ Ⓔ	95. Ⓐ Ⓑ Ⓒ Ⓓ Ⓔ
28. Ⓐ Ⓑ Ⓒ Ⓓ Ⓔ	62. Ⓐ Ⓑ Ⓒ Ⓓ Ⓔ	96. Ⓐ Ⓑ Ⓒ Ⓓ Ⓔ
29. Ⓐ Ⓑ Ⓒ Ⓓ Ⓔ	63. Ⓐ Ⓑ Ⓒ Ⓓ Ⓔ	97. Ⓐ Ⓑ Ⓒ Ⓓ Ⓔ
30. Ⓐ Ⓑ Ⓒ Ⓓ Ⓔ	64. Ⓐ Ⓑ Ⓒ Ⓓ Ⓔ	98. Ⓐ Ⓑ Ⓒ Ⓓ Ⓔ
31. Ⓐ Ⓑ Ⓒ Ⓓ Ⓔ	65. Ⓐ Ⓑ Ⓒ Ⓓ Ⓔ	99. Ⓐ Ⓑ Ⓒ Ⓓ Ⓔ
32. Ⓐ Ⓑ Ⓒ Ⓓ Ⓔ	66. Ⓐ Ⓑ Ⓒ Ⓓ Ⓔ	100. Ⓐ Ⓑ Ⓒ Ⓓ Ⓔ
33. Ⓐ Ⓑ Ⓒ Ⓓ Ⓔ	67. Ⓐ Ⓑ Ⓒ Ⓓ Ⓔ	
34. Ⓐ Ⓑ Ⓒ Ⓓ Ⓔ	68. Ⓐ Ⓑ Ⓒ Ⓓ Ⓔ	

INDEX

REA's Test Preps
The Best in Test Preparation

- REA "Test Preps" are **far more** comprehensive than any other test preparation series
- Each book contains up to **eight** full-length practice tests based on the most recent exams
- **Every** type of question likely to be given on the exams is included
- Answers are accompanied by **full** and **detailed** explanations

REA publishes over 60 Test Preparation volumes in several series. They include:

Advanced Placement Exams(APs)
Biology
Calculus AB & Calculus BC
Chemistry
Computer Science
Economics
English Language & Composition
English Literature & Composition
European History
Government & Politics
Physics B & C
Psychology
Spanish Language
Statistics
United States History

College-Level Examination Program (CLEP)
Analyzing and Interpreting Literature
College Algebra
Freshman College Composition
General Examinations
General Examinations Review
History of the United States I
History of the United States II
Human Growth and Development
Introductory Sociology
Principles of Marketing
Spanish

SAT II: Subject Tests
Biology E/M
Chemistry
English Language Proficiency Test
French
German

SAT II: Subject Tests (cont'd)
Literature
Mathematics Level IC, IIC
Physics
Spanish
United States History
Writing

Graduate Record Exams (GREs)
Biology
Chemistry
Computer Science
General
Literature in English
Mathematics
Physics
Psychology

ACT - ACT Assessment

ASVAB - Armed Services Vocational Aptitude Battery

CBEST - California Basic Educational Skills Test

CDL - Commercial Driver License Exam

CLAST - College Level Academic Skills Test

COOP & HSPT - Catholic High School Admission Tests

ELM - California State University Entry Level Mathematics Exam

FE (EIT) - Fundamentals of Engineering Exams - For both AM & PM Exams

FTCE - Florida Teacher Certification Exam

GED - High School Equivalency Diploma Exam (U.S. & Canadian editions)

GMAT CAT - Graduate Management Admission Test

LSAT - Law School Admission Test

MAT- Miller Analogies Test

MCAT - Medical College Admission Test

MTEL - Massachusetts Tests for Educator Licensure

MSAT- Multiple Subjects Assessment for Teachers

NJ HSPA - New Jersey High School Proficiency Assessment

NYSTCE: LAST & ATS-W - New York State Teacher Certification

PLT - Principles of Learning & Teaching Tests

PPST- Pre-Professional Skills Tests

PSAT - Preliminary Scholastic Assessment Test

SAT I - Reasoning Test

TExES - Texas Examinations of Educator Standards

THEA - Texas Higher Education Assessment

TOEFL - Test of English as a Foreign Language

TOEIC - Test of English for International Communication

USMLE Steps 1,2,3 - U.S. Medical Licensing Exams

U.S. Postal Exams 460 & 470

RESEARCH & EDUCATION ASSOCIATION   **website: www.rea.com**
61 Ethel Road W. • Piscataway, New Jersey 08854 • Phone: (732) 819-8880

Please send me more information about your Test Prep books

Name _____

Address _____

City _____ State _____ Zip _____

REA's Test Prep Books Are The Best!

(a sample of the <u>hundreds of letters</u> REA receives each year)

" I am writing to congratulate you on preparing an exceptional study guide. In five years of teaching this course I have never encountered a more thorough, comprehensive, concise and realistic preparation for this examination. "
Teacher, Davie, FL

" I have found your publications, *The Best Test Preparation...*, to be exactly that. "
Teacher, Aptos, CA

" I used your *CLEP Introductory Sociology* book and rank it 99% — thank you! "
Student, Jerusalem, Israel

" Your *GMAT* book greatly helped me on the test. Thank you. "
Student, Oxford, OH

" I recently got the *French SAT II* Exam book from REA. I congratulate you on first-rate French practice tests. "
Instructor, Los Angeles, CA

" Your *AP English Literature and Composition* book is most impressive. "
Student, Montgomery, AL

" The REA *LSAT* Test Preparation guide is a winner! "
Instructor, Spartanburg, SC

(more on front page)